Two Dry Sods

Tales.. from old Mayo

by Joe Coen

TWO DRY SODS
ISBN-13: 978-1-906628-66-6
Published by CheckPoint Press. Ireland.

www. checkpointpress. com

CheckPoint
Press

Two Dry Sods
Memories of old Mayo

by Joe Coen

Contents

'Two Dry Sods'

This is the title I have given my book which gives an account of my life – as I remember it – from my first memories in 1940 when I was just past my third birthday. I follow this sequence from that time until I leave home on a permanent basis and join the Garda Síochána.

I write this account not because I was unique or that my experiences were very different to the boys who grew up alongside me in the forties and the fifties. The point I want to make is that this lifestyle has changed completely and it is never likely to return. On the other hand my experiences in growing up were little different than those experiences of people in rural areas a hundred years previously.

We ploughed with horses as did my great Grandfather in the 1850s. He sowed some oats and some potatoes as we did. His wife kept hens as did my mother. When the night came on we lit the double wicked lamp just as he did. They went to the fairs to sell cattle as we did.

In the late 1950s the cattle marts had been established and the fairs ended. Ploughing was done with a tractor, and the electricity was connected to the rural houses. Then came the Television, and we saw how other nations did things and we copied them.

The local pub in Kiltimagh is little different to, *"The Rovers Return"* as depicted on the T. V. Even the accents are barely discernible – albeit being mainly of the Irish variety.

Introduction

I write these pieces in the hope that they may entertain older readers who like to be reminded of how we lived long ago. I also hope that some of my younger readers might be interested in the way their fathers and mothers lived. Finally it might be of some interest to have a record of the way life was long ago.

When our people recovered after the great famine of 1847, they embarked on a life style that changed very little until the 1960s. The people, who were actively involved in squeezing a frugal living from a few acres of poor land, are becoming thin on the ground.

Most families kept a small horse, and they joined with a neighbour, and with the two horses they had a team for ploughing and in some cases mowing. In the springtime the fields were ploughed and oats and potatoes were the main crops. Each family kept a few cattle which they reared from birth. They also kept a few cows for milk and butter. Due to the British cheap food policy, it was necessary to diversify, and not to depend upon one source of income. Britain was the only market, and this gave the Irish small farmer a very shaky living.

The Irish small farmer in Mayo in particular was fairly used to hardship over the years and economies evolved which enabled them to make ends meet. In the 1960s the social welfare payments to small farmers were intended to improve their life style. It may have done something to give the housewife money for the supermarket. In one sense these payments degraded the traditional farmer, and it took some of his dignity away. These were tough, proud and hardworking people who should not be forgotten.

In these pages I have ranged over almost seventy years. I never took any notes over these years on any of the matter on which I have written. However I have for over thirty years been writing nostalgic pieces for papers and magazines. I have been a regular contributor to our local parish magazine *Glor Acadmor*. This exercise has enabled me to go back over the years and in this way I have been refreshing my memory. The great energy behind *Glor Acadmor* has been its editor, and general organiser, one Joe Byrne. Many of the pieces in this collection have previously made an appearance in different guises in the local magazine. Joe has given me great encouragement over the years, and I thank him sincerely. I also thank many of my old neighbours who have unwittingly contributed so much towards many of the pieces.

Joe Coen

1

The Beginning

My memories sometimes become confused between what I can actually remember and what I have heard the family relate. I have; however, a few memories which I am sure are what I saw in those far-off times. I saw with my own eyes a two legged white article leaning against the wall of the horse stable. I know that I was standing outside our back door. I also know that we had 'the stations' in the back-end of the year of 1940. At that time I was three years of age. I heard that my Uncle Tom was employed to renovate our house in preparation for the stations, and the two legged article that I had seen outside the stable wall was the new mantle that Tom had made for the stations.

I often heard the family telling how I had misbehaved myself during the stations Mass. Apparently when the bell was rung during Mass I stood up and invited the Priest to ring it again. The adults were mortified at my behaviour, and they seem to enjoy retelling this little incident. I have no independent recollection of this matter. I do know that as a matter of fact I was into bells a bit at the time, for I remember that I had an old brass bell from which the dong had been removed, and so shake as I would, I could get no sound out of it.

The Second World War was raging at the time and I suppose that the toy makers were engaged in making bombs or airplanes. The only toy I remember having was this soundless bell. The fields and the trees and the animals about the farm were my playthings. My dog Bran was a good and loyal friend, and I spent long periods talking to him. He never answered me back, but he seemed to understand what I said to him.

I remember an elderly aunt of my mother's whom we also called Auntie, came to visit us one day. She handed her donkey and cart over to my father, and she ordered that the animal was to be unharnessed and that he was to be tied in the cow house, and given an abundance of sheaves of oats. Having her business attended to, she spread out her two arms and she came towards me to give me a kiss. I was not in favour of kissing at that time and so I made a determined effort to escape. She grabbed the tail of my jacket and pulled me towards her. Bran was just standing about, but when he saw his master being overpowered he stepped in, and he caught the lady's bare leg in a good firm bite, and he was not for letting her go.

She was screaming so loud and shouting in an inarticulate way so that it was a little time before we discovered the cause of the uproar. There were blue marks on her leg and blood was dripping down on to her high laced boots. The dog would have to be put down, and the sooner this was done the sooner would her leg heal. It was said that if the dog was not put down she would lose the use of her leg.

Father was commissioned to act as executioner, and he stalled until the following morning, at which time he would have a suitable cartridge. This was agreed, provided that the dog was locked up. Bran was a most useful dog to keep the neighbours' animals at bay. There was one irregular ass that could terrorise any dog except Bran. I urged Bran to tackle this ass. The ass could kick with either his front or rear legs, and he could destroy any dog if he caught hold of it with his enormous teeth.

He tried his biting trick with Bran, but Bran was too quick for him and he grabbed a hold of the ass's lower lip, and he sunk his teeth and held on, so that the creature turned and fled. So scared was that particular ass that whenever Father whistled at his dog in herding the stock, the poor ass fled to the shelter of his stable.

A shot was fired and almost instantly Auntie's leg improved. She said that it was a remarkable thing that as soon as the dog was dead, her leg got better. Life was good for I had absolute confidence in my dog that he would defend me against man or beast. What Auntie heard and what had actually happened were two different things.

My sister was only one year older than me, but in reality she was almost a generation ahead of me. She had been going to school, and she seemed almost envious of my happy and easy time. In truth when you go to school they will wallop the conceit out of you with a big stick.

I pretended not to take any notice of talk about me going with her to school, but really I was petrified, and I knew that I couldn't bring Bran with me. I told them that I would not go to school and that was an end to it. This was an expression that I had picked up from my father, but somehow the way he said it had more effect.

In the end I had to concede defeat, and I agreed that I would give this school going a shot. As a consolation, the Sunday before I was due at school, my mother took me on a walking tour out to the tarred road, for I had never been out that far. We went past the school and down to a shop. The lady in the shop had a ringing voice, and she called me 'Jew', but she produced a big can of sweets and allowed me to fill my pockets. Sadly I had only one pocket, but she gave me some for my fists as well.

I never forgot her strange-sounding voice, and I always remembered her generosity as well. On our way home, beside the school, we met a group of young men, and one of them was taking photographs, and he showed pictures that he had just taken. I had never heard of such a thing as a camera, and so I did not know that we'd have to wait for many years before the instant camera came along. So when I returned home I could record my experience - I had gone out to the tarred road and I had walked on it. I had been in a shop and I had obtained sweets and finally I had seen a camera. Indeed I felt that I was a kind of an expert on cameras.

I overcame my fear of going to school, and I strode into the school as manfully as possible. The teacher put me sitting at the end of a long desk which was placed at right angles to the other five or six desks. I sat there in silence just taking it all in. When we came in from lunch the teacher asked if I could find my way home, and I made my way home across the fields. This school was not so bad, until one day a boy beside me started to cry and he said that I had twisted his hand. The teacher told him that he was a softie, and I could see her point.

She invited me to go and sit by the fire on the stone fender. I spent most of my time after that sitting by the fire listening to what the teacher was telling the bigger children. Whenever they did not know their lesson I was to go up to them and shout the right answer in their ear. I was also allowed to walk about the room looking at the various exhibits, and I found them interesting.

I could go away home awhile before the rest, and so I was able to carry on with my adventures with Bran, and I had also made friends with the neighbours' ass, and sometimes I used to get him close enough to a heap of stones so that I could get on his back.

My sister was not going very well with the teacher, and then it was decided that we would both go to another school about two miles away. I felt very anxious about this move. In the first place I couldn't find my way home until all of the other children were let out to lead me most of the way home. The teacher was an elderly cranky lady whose nickname was the Gander. After a little while I got on fairly well with her, but the big group of boys coming down the road home used to make life unpleasant for this strange boy from the next parish.

I was happy to return to my own school after about a year, but it had changed too. The kind lady teacher had been sacked, and she was replaced by a local middle aged woman who was like one of the women of the village. Everybody liked her, and we were constantly told how lucky we were to have such a nice teacher. I am left handed and one day she found me with the pen in my left hand. I had not written with my left hand, but she said that I had – a crime of great magnitude. She got red in the face and she began to shout at me and she sent for the master.

We had been warned that he was a fearsome character, and indeed he seemed by his appearance to be so. However he spoke gently to me, and I felt that there was a twinkle in his eye, as he explained that I must in future use my right hand. From that time onwards I did not share the fear which most others had of the master.

When we did move into the master's room we found it so different. No flowers adorned his table or his windows. Life was different out at the master, but as he used to say you will soon get used to the ropes. He seemed to be able to laugh at his own odd ways, and we became accustomed to his strange ways.

2

Two Dry Sods

Ours was a two-teacher school. A lady taught children up to third class, and then the dominant one, the master, taught the boys and girls until they were fourteen years of age. The master had been one of the first formally trained teachers, and he was appointed to take up as principal in our school as his first job. At the time the British were in charge, and most of the teachers were appointed because of their influence with the local landlord or the priests. The story was that the previous head master in our school had been appointed because of his fleetness of foot. The story ran that the landlord's favourite dog had escaped, and this young man outran the dog and returned him to his master. The landlord was so pleased that he had the boy appointed as a teacher. It was observed that the master, even as an old-aged pensioner, could out-run men a quarter of his age.

Now the new master came with proper academic credentials, and he was a model man in every way. He neither drank strong liquor or smoked or used a cane to motivate his charges. Later on he succumbed to all three. He used to be seen in public heavily under the influence of drink, and he regularly smoked cigarettes in school, and his pupils could testify to his prowess with the cane.

He was an old man with white hair when I got to know him. He had a streaky red complexion on a sickly yellow background. There was a lot of loose skin on his face and it seemed to have fallen downwards; his lower lip protruding. He peered owl-like through oval-shaped gold-rimmed spectacles. He never married and his bachelor's life style was clearly evident. His self-centred attitude led him to seem to worry constantly about himself and his health. I can see him standing in front of a blazing fire, his broad-rimmed hat pulled down over his eyes. His "pulls ups", as he always called his cycling trousers, hung loosely on his legs and dangled on the floor. He wore, always, long brown shoes with the toes battered and turning upwards. The smell of the rubberised pull-ups and the smell of his clothing being toasted before the fire were wafted down towards his shivering pupils. Sometimes he would pull his dark grey gabardine coat around his lean stomach with his left hand and he would drive his right hand forward in a physical jerk. He would do this movement a few times and then he would move over to the table. A wave of heat would be felt right down to the back seats once he moved from the front of the fire.

He might crack an egg into his yellow mug with the blue rim. Then he would stab the egg with the point of his pen-knife. He would add milk from the matching yellow jug, and drink this off. Wiser and older people used to say that there was something more in the jug than milk, but we were young and innocent at the time. He would then belch a few times. If he caught one of the girls watching his antics he might crack his joke. He had a full sized photograph of himself at home, and he would bring it to school and she could bring it home and hang it up in the parlour and spend all day Saturday looking at it. Now she had better be minding her tasks.

He had another joke about the time he went to the sports in Castlebar. Some patients from the mental hospital were in attendance at the sports. One of these would look at one of his compatriots and start laughing, in exactly the same way as those pupils down in the desks.

His new bicycle seemed to take on his personality as soon as he got it. He never seemed to be able to afford a carrier on his bicycle. Instead he would order to have one of the brake levers removed to leave the handlebars bare so that he could roll up his coat or his beloved pull-ups around the handlebars. He used to claim that he was six feet in height with good heels. But he always had the saddle down as low as it could go, and off he went pedalling along slowly.

One time he felt a loss of energy, and he made a rule that boys who lived along the Cahir road would run along by his side and push him when the pressure came on going up hills. It was a rare sight to see this big strong looking man sitting low on the bicycle and a small boy running alongside with his little hand on the mudguard of the master's bicycle. The master would keep a sharp look out and if anybody of importance was in the vicinity he would look around at the boy as if to discourage the boy from running after him. Many of the local people were highly amused to see the sight of the pair of them going along the road. A few more serious people felt that a boy whose parents were alive would not be required to do such a menial task. The rule was changed, and he hired the services of a local jaunting car.

The driver of this car was a student at his school and so was under strict orders. The rule was that if the weather was inclement he was to go meet the master near his home. On fine mornings if the wind was blowing from the west his services were not needed. Now sometimes there was no appreciable wind blowing, and so the boy would ride out to meet the master. On one occasion he met the master as the wind was in a favourable position. The master became so angry that he would have to pay the shilling or whatever it was, that he never stopped scolding his driver. The boy's father got wind of this state of affairs and so that enterprise came to halt. From now on he was forced to employ an adult driver with a pony and trap. He would use his bicycle to go home, and he would walk up an incline and then coast along.

For at least forty years he had been travelling along these roads five days a week, and he never became any closer to any of the neighbours who had grown old with him or had attended his school. All you ever got was a cool "Good evening." He was probably a shy man, but he was also very conceited about his learning. He had replaced the old style of school master, and he and his generation of teachers probably looked down on these self-made men. He was in effect a "know-all" and this attitude discouraged many of his pupils from ever trying to develop their education.

I knew a few of the pupils of the older school masters, and even when they were drawing the old-age pension they were still interested in learning new words and how to spell them. Their old school master was forever learning and they followed on his lines. The newly fledged masters knew it all and they never needed to learn any more.

I often think that the master saw himself as fighting against his pupils rather than working with them. He used to take a pride that all the tricks had been tried on him and that no new ones could be thought of. However there was always an enterprising pupil who could teach him a new little lesson.

One year when the school reopened after the summer holidays there was a plague of mice within the school. The little animals would come out when all was quiet and the girls would scream if the mouse went in their direction. The master used to instruct a few of the bigger boys with clogs to stamp on these mice, but the fun was too good so nobody would do any damage to the little creatures. Finally he invested in two mouse-traps. He commissioned a senior boy to take charge of these traps and for every mouse caught there was a bounty of three pence.

For the first few days there was a mouse caught in each trap. Then there was a lull and it appeared that all of the mice had been caught. One more day he announced and the enterprise was over, but then another mouse was caught. This went on for over a week. The boy would go to see his traps and produce the body of the mouse, and draw his bounty.

The hair on the mouse was beginning to fall off and on his inspection of the body the master must have noted this, and so the next morning he sneaked up behind the boy and saw him take the dead mouse out of his pocket and place it in the trap for inspection. The master made no comment, but the scheme was discontinued.

He took his work very seriously, sometimes too seriously. A boy, who might have failed to answer a simple question in his religious knowledge for the inspector, might still be capable of doing useful work. The master would always see this boy as he who failed to answer a simple question. When that same boy grew to be a man he might be trusted to direct operation in a construction site that would cover half the parish. He might not still be too sure of how to spell "their", meaning belonging to them, but he'd have clerks in his office who could do menial jobs like that.

I had witnessed the master using the cane to a point where he would feel that he had exhausted himself. I had never seen him punish anybody unjustly. He was a great teacher and he never spared himself in patiently explaining every detail. At such time if any of his pupils were seen by him to be gawking up at Edward Frain who was doing his work in the fields then heaven have mercy on the pupil for the master had none. He was generous with money, and he would frequently offer a half crown as a prize for the best effort at composition or for a test in arithmetic.

I remember on one such test I qualified for the prize, but because I had been found in disgrace I was penalised. Someone had chewed the wooden end of his steel pen so that it became a kind of little brush. I was fascinated by this instrument and I used it to write the pupil's name on the back of their shirt. I was found out and I was given a scolding for wasting my time. Later on the master decided that I was to forfeit the prize except that he gave me tuppence ha'penny in a heap of half pennies. I became so angry that I grabbed the coppers and threw them on the table in front of him. He just took the coins, put them in his pocket and said not a word.

The local adult population had some idea that the Department of Education provided funds to pay for the cost of cleaning and heating the school. It was also well known that whatever this fund was used for it was not used for cleaning or heating the school. In my time in school we were on a rota to sweep the floor. The window sills or other woodwork never got a rub. He wiped down his table himself, for he could never get any pupil to do it properly. Sweeping the school floor was good fun. You kicked the wainscoting and the cast-iron legs of the old desks, and generally made as much noise as you possible could. We could recognise the angry expression on the master and mischievously we enjoyed getting under his skin. He could put up with our noise or do it himself. Sometimes he'd take the handle of the brush in one hand and pull the brush towards his feet rather like a man might be gathering hay to make a small hay cock.

"You'd never see your mother pushing the brush in front of her," he'd say with the nearest thing to a smile he ever gave. I certainly never saw my mother pulling the brush towards her in the way that he demonstrated. We would waste as much time as possible sweeping, and suddenly he'd shout stop. In regard to sweeping he was easy enough to please.

The heating was a matter which he took more seriously. The rule was that each family brought a load of turf before Christmas and another load after Christmas. To supplement this each pupil was required to bring two dry sods of turf to school each morning. My father felt it was his duty to bring one horse cart load of turf to the school each year. One time when my father was tipping the load of turf outside the school gate the master dropped out to have a word with him. "A fine load of good turf," was the greeting which he gave to my father. My father had been taught by the same man when he was a younger teacher. The master sniffed a few times

18

and then he said, "The rule is that you bring one load of turf before Christmas and another load after Christmas."

Concealing any fear he might still have for his old master my father said, "Well I have just made a new rule and this is all the turf you will get this year, and if every family brought that much you would have a good fire."

The master looked sharply at my father and then he legged it into the school like a wounded old turkey cock.

Next morning he nabbed my sister going into the school without her two dry sods. She was caught by my father the following morning taking two sods of turf from the reek and she told the story. From that morning she used to sneak off with her two sods unknown to my father. I never brought two sods or indeed any sod. I used to linger in the shelter of Frain's bushes until the queer fellow had gone into school and then I'd hurry on down and give two good kicks with my clogs to the wainscoting which signalled that I had thrown in my quota of two sods. Very few of the boys ever brought a sod of turf to school, but the girls were more timid or perhaps liked to be in his good graces and they would be seen with their two dry sods.

3

Using a Bicycle

The musical sound that comes from a bicycle as it is ridden free-wheel down an incline is forever with me. The first time that I became aware of this magical music I was seated close to the back wheel of the machine. I was sitting on the carrier of a bicycle which my father was riding. He was taking me to a sports meeting a few miles from our home. I have been told where the field is, but I have no memory of the sports. All that I can remember is the whirring sound that came from the back wheel of the bicycle. Even these times, whenever I ride a bicycle, I love to hear that sound.

I was about four years of age when I first experienced this delightful ride on a bicycle. At that time bicycles were a treasured possession. They were expensive and they were also very hard to come by. The emergency was in full swing during the Second World War. Bicycles and parts for them were scarce, and people were so pleased to be able to get any parts and so they did not haggle about the price. The "gombeen men" were in their hey-day.

I often heard talk of a spanking new bicycle which the local parish priest got at the time. He wanted to show that it behoved all citizens to spare petrol to help the allies. There was only one other motor car in the parish and it was used by the dispensary doctor. In any event the priest only took one spin on his new machine and it was never seen again, although there were a few parishioners on the look-out for a good second hand bicycle.

In our house there were two bicycles, but my father had to cannibalise his own machine in order to have parts for my

20

mother's bicycle. There was therefore one bicycle in our house and it was on this that I first started to ride. There was a narrow road leading downhill from our house out to a tarred road. My first venture was to stand on the pedals and let the bicycle coast down the hill. I had only a few falls until I learnt to steer the bicycle. Then I would walk back up the hill and try this again. A few times I managed to put the pedals half-way round, and then on one glorious day I succeeded in pushing the pedals the whole way round.

The little road from our house to the main road bore all the signs of its usage. The tracks of the horse's hooves had kept a narrow path free of grass on the centre. The two wheels of vehicles had cleared the grass off two narrow margins. There were two ribbons of grass running along the road. They might look very picturesque on a postcard, but for an inexperienced cyclist these grass ribbons presented a problem. The trick was if you started off in one of these margins you should not try to get out of them for fear of a skid. I learned this too from experience.

Now I felt that I was fit to sally forth out to the main public road. The fairly smooth tarred road allowed me to reach much higher speeds, and sometimes I would listen to the musical sound when I free-wheeled. I got up a good speed and then I swung in our own road. Up to this time I had not discovered that you needed to take precautions when turning, and so I bumped into the loose stone wall which repulsed me and I was thrown on to the centre of the road with the bicycle on top of me.

I remember thinking that I must have broken my leg, and then I thought of the condition of the bicycle. My leg would get well, but what about the bicycle? Then I saw my friend Johnnie, a neighbour. He took my hand and lifted me up and I realised that I was not too bad, but what about the bike? He pacified me and he began work on the repairs and somehow he got the two wheels running and I very carefully wheeled the bicycle in and I left it in its usual parking place at the gable end of the house.

I swore that I would never again take the bicycle, but parents were very understanding then too. In less than a week I was off again cycling and before long I was using the bicycle to run messages to the shop. I used the first money that I earned to buy myself a second hand bicycle. I remember that old machine. It had no carrier or extra weights. It seemed to have been put together especially for speed. I used to stoop my head down to the high handlebars, and in this I felt that I had the same advantages of a low racing bicycle. I was not so good on the grass, but on the road I could keep up with the best of them.

I still ride a bicycle and I remember all of the lessons that I have learnt over the years. I have become too cute to ever attempt taking a corner at high speed. The one pleasure that I still enjoy is the sound of the free-wheel as I coast down an incline. Somehow the sound is not as clear as it used to be.

4

The Black Mare

I have a picture of that noble animal etched into my mind. She walked tall and she held her head high. Her coat was a shiny black, with a splash of white on her face and she had two white socks on her front legs. I used to be put astride her broad back when she was harnessed to go ploughing. At such times I would hold tight to the tops of the hames. It was a bit nerve racking for me when she took a drink at the pond for she would raise her head high enough to throw back her collar.

I remember the last spin I had on her back on the evening before Father brought her to the fair in Claremorris. I had to hold on for dear life to her coarse mane. She had become very fat, and my short legs were of little use to me in balancing on her broad back. The mare had become sick and her illness was almost like it had affected a member of the family. She had earned the right to a dignified retirement, but times were hard, and as my father used to say, "Beggars cannot be choosers." So Father brought our fine animal to the fair and he sold her to a gentleman horse dealer named Barney Spellman.

Barney was looking over the mare after he had bought her. "You trotted her fairly hard on the way to here."
"Yes I did," said my father. "She trotted all the whole of the ten miles to here and she pulled me along also on the bike."
"She is a bit swollen of her front quarters - her heart is not so good. She is a beautiful looking animal and anyway, I buy to sell again," said Barney.

Father knew how magnificent she looked and he would have kept her if he could. Now he was on the lookout for a replacement. He went to the fair in Kilkelly a few times but he could find nothing to compare with the black mare. I suspect that the ten pounds that he got for her had been whittled away, and now he had a bog road to complete, and he had stones to cart from the sandpit a few hundred yards away. I suppose that if he could finish the road he would be in funds again.

A relative had a disreputable looking beast that had been grazing up in the bog in Annach a dhoithe. If this creature got feeding he might be able to draw the stone and gravel to finish the road. The previous owner had grown to detest this unfortunate beast, and I would guess that the bargain was easily made at a very low price. This new purchase was said to be very quiet, and in this sense I sort of looked forward to seeing it. It was a brown coloured horse with a very big grey head. This was not a horse, but a mule. My own youthful tongue could never get around the word and so I always referred to the animal as the "muler". Father had christened him Isaac or to be more precise ould Isaac.

Soon we learned that Isaac was thin because his back teeth were worn and so he could not eat hay or any other sort of fodder properly. So poor old Isaac never grew fat, and he contented himself wandering around eating soft branches off fancy shrubs. He had a habit of wandering to where outlying cattle might be fed. He could not eat much himself, but he would not allow any other creature neither horse nor bovine to eat either. He would beat them away with kicks and bites with his long yellow front teeth.

Our nearest neighbour Tom farmed in a somewhat unorthodox manner, and sometimes he would give his animals, twenty-four hours or on occasions a forty eight hours ration. Our Isaac would commandeer all of these rations. When Tom would return home often late at night in the days before the ESB or fridges were known in our locality, he would go out and milk a pint or two from old Polly, a quiet old cow.

In his searching about in the dark to find old Polly, Tom might leave his hand on Isaac's back to be rewarded by a savage screech and an attempt to kick. Tom had faced the terror of the British Army, but he was no match for old Isaac in the dark.

Whenever Tom met me conveying the mule back to our territory, he would make a generous offering to encourage me to keep the animal at home. In fact Tom's efforts were counterproductive. In my youthful and sinful way I would open the gate and Isaac would amble off back up the road towards the rations which Tom had laid for his own stock.

I am sure that Father missed the stylish mare and the dash he could cause with her trotting along with her head in the air. Her replacement was at the other end of the scale. There was something in the matter of status, about a mule in that he was lower down the scale than a donkey. A man driving a donkey might also have one or two horses at home. A mule or a jennet was a statement of the means of a man in a rural community. There was one positive aspect in this demotion for Father. He himself would be required to take charge of the mare, but the lad – even at five years of age – could be left in charge of old Isaac.

So from now I was the horseman in the family. I could go into the field and catch old Isaac and harness him and yoke him into the cart. He had rules of his own though. You had to follow a certain ritual when dressing him. In the ordinary way the collar and hames would be put on and the cart straddle and finally the breech. Not so with Isaac. You dared not put on the straddle unless you had the breech on first. If you put on the straddle without the breech, Isaac would hold his head down to the ground and kick as high as he could for as long as he was able.

25

I gained wide experience of horse-driving, and I also learned to have a healthy respect for these animals. Whenever merchandise was required from the town or village I was called upon with my wagon. The pace was slow and nothing would prevail upon Isaac to increase his own set pace. A few times Father took over the reins and he applied pressure by means of a stout stick, but the only effect was that the animal would shake its tail. The poor old creature had taken all the beatings that his former owners could give, and he could do no more. Yet he was strong, and he shifted full horse-cart loads of gravel and stone. To be fair I'd say that Father pulled most of the load himself and that old Isaac just kept the shafts of the cart up off the ground. The horse cart was too big for him and when the wheels went into a rut, the big cart would send the poor old thing staggering.

But when we got a nice light donkey cart for him, he looked a bit better, but his speed did not increase. I had seen a man with a pony and trap and he used a light whip. I got a light stick and I tied a leather boot-lace on to the top of the stick, and I used to let on that if I applied this whip that Isaac would and could go like the wind. Later when we got a good ass, I was an expert. All the tricks had been tried on me by old Isaac. Observers never took any notice of a boy driving an ass in those times, but old Isaac did attract some more attention.

"Where are you off to with old Dunlop?" one observer used to remark. He seemed to think that he was a bit smart, and I used to ignore remarks like that. The fact that most of the harness upon the old mule was made from worn bicycle tyres was none of his business.

I remember one wet day my father undertook to make a straw collar for old Isaac. The horse's collar was so big for him that it was hitting him on the knees as he walked. A few sheaves of oats were scotched off the end wall of the shed, and this straw was used to make plaits. These plaits were soaked in water and then they were hammered flat with a lump of timber. The mule was paraded and a few measurements were taken of his neck and shoulders. The collar was of a circular shape coming into a point at the top. There was no opening on the top; of the collar like the conventional model. The plaits of straw were stitched together with string, and when about a half a dozen layers were neatly fitted together, the mule was called for a fit on.

At this point there was no lining or backing on the collar. Father took a firm hold of the collar with his two hands, and he attempted to push the collar over the animal's ears. Try as hard as he could he could not get the collar over the mule's two ears. Father was a strong, determined man and he set about putting on this collar with a will. He and the mule did a fair bash at square dancing, but to no avail. In one last heave, Father put his shoulder against the beast's head and so the mule went into reverse and his hind legs were pushed up on to a bank. There sat the mule with his two front legs up straight in front of him somewhat like a dog sometimes sits at the fire. One of the mule's ears was caught under the collar and the other one was free.

Apparently pleased to be left unmolested, the mule just sat there. I have never heard of a mule to smile, and God knows the poor beast had little enough to smile about, but I felt sure that I could discern a twinkle in his big brown eyes. Rather than run the risk of being found with any trace of a smirk, I beat a hasty retreat. Later when I got the smell of tobacco smoke, I ventured up close again. The mule was still sitting where I had seen him with his collar half on and half off. I was about to approach him to remove the collar when my mother came on the scene.

She admired the way that the collar was made, and she marvelled at the skill Father had shown in his stitching.
"Aye it's grand, but I can't get the bleddy thing over his big head."

27

"I think that I used to see the lads and Uncle Jim turning the collar upside down to get it over the animal's head, and then turn it back again before it goes down over his shoulders."

I remember that Father left his pipe on the low wall of the pig sty, and then he turned the collar as Mother had suggested, and the collar slipped on as easily as you'd put on your cap – a piece of cake really.

5

Bonfires

The early summer used to be a tedious time for the schoolboy. In school the master was crowding us with matters which he claimed we should have done early in the spring. At home there was the usual rush of work and special chores were left out for the boy. One of the most soul-destroying of these jobs was picking stones off the meadow. This job was usually left aside until the grass had grown so long that the stones could no longer be seen. I remember diligently searching for these stones, and having the top of the sod fences strewn with bucketfuls of small stones, and the boss would just walk up the field about twenty yards and collect a fistful of stones so that they would not destroy the edge of his blade.

Collecting combustible materials for the bonfire was a great relief. The bonfire was on the eve of St John's, the 23rd of June, and any time after the first of May we began collecting. Furze bushes were there to cut in almost any man's land, but they had to be cut, which was tough work on a youth with a bad saw or a blunt hatchet.

Motor tyres were the boys for the bonfire, if you could lay hands on them, but they were very scarce in those times. Strong well-seasoned branches of any tree were valuable as a combustible. Faded branches that were left to fill gaps in fences were very handy for us but some farmers were most unreasonable, and they often objected. They were not able to see that a big bonfire added greatly to the status of the locality. The bigger the bonfire the farther away it could be seen, and thus gave valuable publicity to the village. Some people refused to believe this.

Once I was caught red-handed dragging a great haw-thorn bush along the road. Although I was dropping sweat, the irate farmer ordered me to go back and leave that bush where I found it. Later on when I was returning empty-handed, and I saw that the farmer had cooled down. I put the case that 'St Patrick once got into trouble for daring to light a bonfire before the High King had lit his own'.
"St Patrick won't run after my cattle if they break out during the summer," He replied.

At the time I could see that there was no hope of arguing with a man of that frame of mind. If I had known at the time I could have used a better argument. For bonfires go back to the first civilised man in Ireland. In Keating's *The History of Ireland* there is an account of how the Fianna used to light great fires on selected sites. They would send some boys back to this site with their first kill. A great fire would be lit and stones heated, and these stones would be thrown into a trough of water. Into this trough they would place some meat to be cooked. Experiments have shown that it takes about a half an hour for these stones to bring the water in the trough to boiling.

Investigations have shown that the Fianna used to make up their beds nearby the fire. They used to spread out light branches on the ground and cover them with moss, and then place some rushes on the beds to lie on. Indeed all of these materials were readily available to us, but the idea just never occurred to us. These ancient cooking places as they are sometimes called are plentiful around the country.

I have heard of a few attempts to domesticate, as it were, the bonfire. A large pot was procured and set upon the fire in which it was hoped some pleasant vitals might be cooked. On another occasion a musician was prevailed upon to bring his musical instrument and to perform.

Unfortunately in those times bonfires seemed to attract a few vandals. To these people a pot set on the fire or a musician playing his music, presented nothing more to them than a cock-shot. Some of these afore-mentioned people, had developed great skill in the throwing of half-burnt sods of turf up into the air. They could by sheer physical exertion propel a lighted sod sixty feet into the air for the sole pleasure of seeing it drop, in tongues of fire, onto the head of some innocent guest.

In earlier times the site for a bonfire was selected on the highest hill in the locality. In Bruff the site was on the top of Kenny's hill overlooking the Aghamore road. Later on perhaps to accommodate the motoring public the sites were selected at a crossroads or on a wide spot on the road away from dwellings. For some reason, the visibility of a bonfire from afar was no longer a compelling factor. However the fire-throwers seemed to follow the bonfires, whether up on a hill or on the side of the road.

I remember an occasion when a number of motor cars were parked a safe distance from the fire. The vandals were at their work and a half-burnt sod of turf came down on the bonnet of a car, perhaps not in tongues of fire, but with an awful thud. The car owner ran immediately and grabbed the sod and threw it in front of his vehicle. Then he stood up to his full height and puffed out his chest, and shouted that he would give ten bob to the man who threw the sod if he would come back and pick it up. Unfortunately there were no takers, for a boxing match even in bare knuckles would have added greatly to the festivities.

The availability of motorised transport enabled people interested in attending bonfires to travel distances to see how bonfires in other districts were conducted. On one such occasion we were just in time to a witness a performance which greatly increased the entertainment at least as far as we were concerned. A tall strapping young man stepped

31

forward and addressed another young man who was accompanied by three or four athletic young men.

It appeared that the performer was on his home ground, and the small group had come prepared for any encounter that might occur. The small group was being spoken to and warned of his previous pugilistic achievements, in Ireland and also overseas. The visitors were more modest in that they spoke but very little of their powers, but did warn of what might happen if any blows were struck.

As a warning this aggressor removed his immaculate black serge jacket, and he threw it on the dusty sand road, and he stamped on it a few times leaving the imprint of his dusty shoes on the beautiful garment. Then he pulled off his tie and he let it off with the wind. Then he ripped off his white shirt sending buttons flying in all directions. Now properly ready for any encounter, he danced forward to meet his foe, but he stopped short.

"Just hit me once, Paddy," were the only words from the visitor, but they were spoken with a warning. The aggressor danced away a bit and he came forward once more, but he made no contact. He must have spotted the lady, on whose behalf he was prepared to fight, was moving away from the scene accompanied by the smallest and most emaciated little man in the locality. The sight seemed to have brought this fighting man to his senses, for he picked up his jacket and dusted it down with repeated slaps of his enormous hand. His opponent had located his tie and shirt and stood nearby ready to hand them back. We were denied any further show for the night.

Law makers seem to have an eye on bonfires. Almost one hundred and fifty years ago a law was passed which purported to prevent fires from being lit within fifty feet of a public road. It seems that the will of the people prevailed. Now we have more stringent laws which prevent smoke unless it comes through a chimney. It is not easy to have a fire without smoke.

Country people and outdoor workers seem content enough to cook and eat their meals indoors. However city people and people who work indoors seem to have a hankering to cook and eat out of doors. To meet this need the barbeque was invented.

Recently I was present when one of these barbeques was in operation. It was a simple griddle with a few steaming pieces of charcoal, slowly sizzling a few over-sized sausages. The smell was good and the food tasted moderately good. There was no atmosphere. When I remember the cheering and good humoured banter of the bonfires of long ago I could have cried, but that was not allowed. I was sorely tempted to grab one of the charcoals and try my hand at fire throwing, but when I looked at the guests sitting sedately on their deck-chairs with their flip-flops dangling on their toes, I realised that it was time for me to go home.

6

A Little Gratuity

As a young lad growing up in the wide open countryside, I never lacked for matters that interested me. However there used to be a few days around the Christmas when I would be a little disappointed. I used to write to Santa Claus early in the month of November, listing the items that I expected. A local boy a few years older than me, had a train set, that when fully assembled would go round and round on the little tracks. The same boy had a toy motor car that when he wound it up, would go around the kitchen floor. He also had a pair of roller skaters the likes of which I had never seen or heard of before. Any one of such items would have satisfied me, for I was not a greedy fellow. But alas Santa seemed to be on strike or at least on a "go slow".

The greatest toy that I had ever seen was a crossbow. I was allowed to take the precious weapon in my hands but I was not allowed to shoot with it. I took careful note of how it was made. The main barrel was made of a piece of round wood about an inch and a half in thickness and about two feet long. I knew where such wood was growing in our garden. The inner soft material could be scooped out with a piece of wire. This formed the barrel, but the bow was made of a steel rod almost as thick as a pencil. The perfect piece of steel for the job was a stay, out of a man's umbrella.

The only men that I had seen carrying umbrellas was the local doctor, when he came to the school. The other individual just as remote from me was the local parish priest. Now how could I approach either of these gentlemen and ask them if they intended to throw away their umbrella. I made plans that I would approach the parish priest one Saturday and see if he had an old umbrella in his shed, but, coward that I am, I baulked at the last minute. I kept the matter in mind and about twenty years later, I saw an old umbrella trampled down in the tar on the edge of the road. I picked it up, and it was the real thing, but now I have no use for a crossbow anymore. The crossbow was deadly accurate and it would discharge a missile about a foot long. The ordinary bow I had often made out of a piece of an ash plant. A branch of ash was not acceptable; it had to be the original growth of a young tree.

The first year's growth of elderberry tree or 'boltree' as we used to call it, was a most versatile timber for the young country boy. The inner soft white material could be poked out and the cylinder could be used to make whistles or smaller toy guns. A whistle could easily be made by stuffing one end with a cork or a piece of a sally rod. The mouth piece was made in the following way. Half an inch from the top you made a cut half way across the tube. Moving down the tube about half an inch you made a cut beginning very shallow and going until you met the first cut. Now you fixed a half cork on the top, and sometimes you might have to adjust the cut or the cork slightly until you got a shrill whistle. The bigger the bore of the cylinder, the louder was the sound of the whistle.

This same first year's growth of elderberry was also useful for making a small gun that would shoot a match accurately up to twenty feet. You selected a piece of this wood about a foot long. Near about the centre you cut a slot three inches long. Now you got the spring of a clock, and about six inches of this was fixed into the slot. To set the thing you pulled back the spring, and then a touch of your finger and off it went. The finding of the spring of a clock necessitated a wide search, and sometimes it was impossible, for clocks were not being dumped, but were being repaired over and over again. There was another source of good quality springs used in the inner garments worn by stylish ladies. Sometimes a thorough search of an outbuilding often yielded a find of a few of these springs. Like the gentlemen with the umbrellas you could not so well ask a lady if she had recently discarded one of her inner garments. While the privileged few youngsters enjoyed playing with their toys, I suspect that they also cherished the idea they were so much luckier than the rest of us. Nevertheless our deprivation at Christmas time also encouraged our resourcefulness, and to this day I enjoy improvising.

The people in our house used to be forever making excuses for Santa. "Sure where could he get toys in these times, aren't all the toy makers now working on making aeroplanes for the war."

I must admit that aeroplanes interested me a lot in those times. I often counted ten or twelve of them flying over our house. I heard my father saying that it was the "Yanks that were taking a short cut across the country to throw bombs on the German ships out in the Atlantic." The English and the Germans too respected our neutrality, but the Yanks took the short cut.

I used to draw a picture of an aeroplane on the concrete floor of our kitchen, with a piece of whitewash chipped off the wall. My pictures were not complete for I had never seen any aeroplane except those that flew over our house. I did my best and I never missed any aeroplane, and I observed until it was out of sight. I was hoping that sometime a plane would come down so that we could have a proper look at it. There was it appears a real possibility that one of these planes would visit us on some occasion. There was one big field in our parish and it was judged to be big enough to land an aeroplane. The local parish priest led a group of busy parish citizens and they buried tar-barrels with half of them sticking up. This idea purported to make it impossible for a plane to land.

A few of the local farmers dug up some of the barrels to use for mixing spray for their potatoes. The idea was to discourage the Germans from visiting us. I would not have cared whether it was a German or American or a British plane that came down just so that I could have a good look at it.

While there were many dull moments in our lives on the ground there were often little incidents that gave us great pleasure. Such a mundane act as letting out the pigs often created periods of high levity at least for the young people. We usually kept about five pigs, and in the housing arrangements which we had for them, it was necessary to release the pigs while the pig sty was swept out. A pig that has been confined for long periods usually acts in the following manner; he will move out of his domain very cautiously for a few steps, let out a grunt and jump up with all four legs off the ground, and then off he'll go at a surprising speed for an animal so ungainly looking.

I used to enjoy these antics of the pigs, and if the gate was open they would scamper off into the open fields. Sometimes they would roll their bodies in the long grass in pure delight. At the end of this field there was a well which overflowed out onto the land, and this was an absolute heaven for the pigs. They would root and roll until they looked like real black pigs. Their fun was so good that it was hard to entice them back to their place of confinement. Rattling the handle of the bucket seemed to have lost its virtue. To drive a pig is a task not to be engaged in lightly. Usually the only solution was to wait until they became hungry, and then they would return uninvited. Afterwards precautions were taken to ensure that the gate was bolted, and once or twice I slipped it open, and got myself into a lot of trouble.

Some of the animals seem to have had traits that have been lost in their modern equivalent. In those days some cows used to love to browse along little streams and then go into the stream and feast on the soft green grass that grows in such places. In due course the cow would sink into the soft bottom, and be unable to get out. This happened frequently, and so a meitheall of the neighbours would arrive with ropes and spades and levers to help the cow out of her predicament.

A horse in such a predicament was a much more exciting event, for a horse is a nervous creature, and it will jump and plunge, and can be dangerous. It appears that a horse needs to have its head free before it can make an attempt to get out. The first order used to be, "Get on his head."

Two strong men were required to keep the horse's head down while the others tied ropes on to its legs and body. Each man had his own way of how properly to do this work, and it was exciting to hear these grown-ups coming close to having a boxing round or two.

I never hear of cows going bogging any more, I suppose that if they do, the farmer will just yoke up his tractor to them and pull them out, without any of the commotion of long ago. Perhaps the cows have evolved a bit too. Long ago cows often poked the soil off the potato pit and began to gobble down the potatoes, and then almost invariably one had a potato stuck in her gullet. This was a regular feature of country life and we were all prepared for such an eventuality. The younger boys ran for help. You needed two stout men to hold the cow in situation.

The local cow doctor in my time was gone past his prime and since he never rode a bicycle we used to have to wait for him to make his way across the fields. The only instrument that he ever carried with him was a few feet of a rubber hose. Tongs were provided locally, for every house had such an implement for stoking up the fire. That, and a good big tough sod of turf, was all that was needed, and there was no shortage of such essential pieces of equipment. The two strong men opened the cow's mouth and the expert laid the tongs across its tongue. Now there was a further need for brawn to get the cow's mouth open sufficiently to wedge in the sod of turf between the two legs of the tongs.

When the cow's mouth was locked open, the cow doctor used his piece of rubber hose to poke the potato down the cow's neck. Sometimes, however it was not possible to dislodge the blockage and so the brave man was forced to insert his bare hand into the cow's mouth and down her throat to remove the obstacle by hand. Little the worse for her experience the cow waddled off to try eating grass. Cows are such placid creatures. Sometimes the owner of the cow would treat the grown-ups with a bottle of stout, and then to stories of cows and horses, and strong men. In the present times the cows, the horses and the men are but mere shadows of those of the olden days. Looking back I would not have swapped these experiences, and the joy and excitement and the telling afterwards, and the feeling that one was a part of this great, exciting life.

7

Wren-boys

There are two kinds of wren-boys. One is where accomplished musicians and dancers go from house to house to entertain the householders and to enjoy themselves. There is also another kind of wren-boy; boys of school-going age, who put on a mild disguise and go from house to house collecting money. Wren-boys of this latter kind, never disguise themselves so much that they wouldn't be easily recognised. Recognition almost always increases the size of the stipend that they receive. They, all of them carry light musical instruments such as tin whistles or mouth-organs. Few of these wren-boys can play any music, but they use the instrument to alert the householders of their arrival.

I was no more than six years of age when I first attempted to go out with the wren-boys. I arranged with a local boy that we'd go out, and he was to call down to our house. I waited all day, but he never showed up. He told me later that he was going out the front door when he was captured. His mother had some qualms about letting her son go out begging, as she euphemistically put it.

My own parents did not seem to have any qualms about letting me out on such a mission. The next year I prepared in good time. I couldn't sleep on the night before the event. Early the next morning I set off across the fields to meet my partner, and he had gone to meet me along the road. I can still recall the kindly young neighbour, who spotted the lone wren-boy going along the road, and he alerted me so that we met up.

I carried a home-made whistle. For weeks in advance I had been fashioning whistles, and I selected that which produced the loudest call. I made these whistles out of a second year's growth of the elderberry bush. You selected a straight piece about six inches long, and poked the soft spongy material out of the centre thus leaving a hollow cylinder. One of the old-fashioned steel knitting needles was the perfect instrument for this job. A triangular cut was made about an inch from the top. The opening at the top was half closed with a cork. The bottom was then plugged. Some minor adjustments might have to be made to the triangular cut to regulate the tone. This instrument did not produce music!

My pal was not into woodwork, but he persuaded his mother when decapitating the goose for Christmas to make the incision close to the bird's eyes, thus saving its windpipe. This organ was removed intact from the carcase. It had pieces of red meat still hanging on, and it was about a foot long. Although as a musical wind instrument it was a little revolting, it was nevertheless a versatile instrument that could produce a great variety of sounds, remotely like a brass band, but more particularly like a flock of geese.

Many of the grown-ups showed an interest in our musical instruments. Many of them took my whistle and blew it, and they got me to tell them how it was made. They stood back a little from the other instrument. Some asked if it was still alive, and others closer to the mark claimed that it was giving off a stink smell. None made so bold as to blow into it. They laughed at us and some said that we sounded a bit like Mick Del and his band. We were laughing too.

Going out with the wren-boys was considered slightly amusing, by the adult population, but we, the participants took the business very seriously. Gathering money is always a serious business. As the years went by our legs grew longer and stronger, and so we were able to travel much farther from home.

My partner had a special pocket sewn into his trousers, so that our money could not be easily removed from us. We were trusting wee fellows, and so we made no secret of the manner in which we had concealed our money, or that we put all of our money in the one basket so to speak. We had got an early start, at about 9am. We judged that there would be at least one person up in each house, and they would have some small change left out for the wren-boys. We had judged correctly and so by about two o'clock in the afternoon we had the pocket almost full. We were set upon by a lone wren-boy. Our plan was that we would run in opposite directions, but our assailant had good information and he knocked down my pal and had the money gone in the wink of an eye.

Sadly we returned home penniless, but we were fortified with a good slice of Christmas cake. The old folk took our robbery very seriously, and they sent scouts out on bicycles to trace this big lone wren-boy. Foolishly he came strolling up the road right into the hands of my pal's father, who had some experience of police work in a part amateur way. He challenged the big wren-boy, who denied all knowledge of ever having seen us. I was beginning to believe him when the man took him and immersed him head first into the barrel of freezing water.

The big boy's money fell out on to the footpath and we were ordered to pick it up. After a second dip in the barrel the boy began to sing as they say in the USA. I felt guilty about taking his money as well as our own, but I did what I was ordered to do. From that time onwards we carried stout sticks, which we were fully prepared to use, but we never got a chance. The experience has left me with great sympathy for any person who has ever been robbed.

Once we left our own area where we were known, we often got a frosty enough reception. Taunts heard like: "Did ye have a good year at the hay?"

This was a reference to the practise in those days of young men and boys going across to England to work for farmers over there. I can recall one bitter old fellow who refused to part with even the smallest sum, but he shouted after us, "Beyond in England ye should be."

Like any good professionals we were never deterred by such comments so long as the money kept coming. Our collections were rarely for our own personal use, so we could take such insults on the chin. The cause which I remember we collected for each year was to buy a new football for the school.

Growing up too fast was a serious handicap, but we could have prolonged our days as wren-boys had we the dedication to learn how to play any musical instrument. Thinking of it now I am surprised that we did not turn to singing, for it would not have taken too long to learn a few verses of a song. I still feel a tinge of regret that I was forced to retire from the ranks of the wren-boys prematurely.

8

Becoming Useful

I have a very clear memory of my seventh birthday. My mother could improvise and create a feast out of almost nothing at all. At the time of my seventh birthday "the Emergency" was in full swing. We had the black flour and sugar was rationed. Nevertheless my mother sieved the flour through a silk stocking, and so we had the nearest thing that I had ever seen to white flour. Somehow she scraped up a few extra cups of sugar, and with some cocoa and lots of eggs she made a chocolate layer cake. This was baked on the open fire, and she used to pour a little hot water from the kettle into the mug with sugar and then she added the cocoa, and she kept mixing this until it was a creamy substance that could be consumed without any cake at all. However this was plastered onto two flat cakes and left there to set and cool.

I was aware that this preparation was being made in my name to be feasted upon when our day's work was done. This was my first day at real work. We had forty lea-land ridges each over a hundred yards long. We brought out about five bags of slits or seed potatoes in the cart pulled by Isaac, and deposited them on the headland. Father had a new 'steeveen', a pointed stake, and he began to make three holes across the ridge. Each row of holes was about fifteen or sixteen inches apart. I had a small bucket into which I had scooped some of the seed potatoes. I followed Father dropping a potato into each hole that he had made. After he had finished one ridge he walked back and started again on the second ridge. When we had five or six ridges sown, we began to quench the holes or cover the potatoes with a little sod or a small amount of clay on the top of the spade. I just quenched one row of the holes and Father did the other two.

44

"Cover them well, he advised, for the crows sitting on that ash tree are watching us and if we give them half a chance they will come and steal our potatoes."After about an hour my sister came along and she eased the work a bit on me, and she also gave an up-to-date report on the chocolate cake. At dinner time my father gave both my sister and me glowing reports on how good we were at working. From now on he would have his own help and not be depending upon neighbours for help with two- men jobs. From that day onwards I was counted on the strength of the workers on the farm. I remember that feeling of fatigue that came over me when I sat down in the evening, but I was able to enjoy the feast that we had on the chocolate cake.

Later that year I was up on the loads of hay tramping them down and doing my best to make loads of hay. Sometimes the corner would fall off the load en route to the stack garden. I could tell by the look on my father's face that he was disappointed in me. It did not occur to me to say that I was doing my best, because in the circumstances my best was not good enough. More by good luck sometimes I'd make a good load, but there was slow progress.

I was beginning to feel that I never would be able to make a proper load. Some turned out fairly good but some looked horrible, and I'd be keeping my fingers crossed that the load would reach the garden before it fell off. I used to keep my eyes and ears open to see if I could discover the secret of making a good load every time. Then one day Father and I went up to my uncle's place to help in bringing home their hay. Their hay field was a few miles away from their haggard, and it behoved the loader to make a good load that would ride all the way to the haggard. The first load that I made didn't fall, but it looked a very poor specimen compared to the load made by Tommie Carney. From then onwards Tommie made all the loads, and I was assigned to building the hay in the shed.

While my father was forking up the hay to Tommie I could hear Tommie giving directions. "I can't deal with that big forkful," he said and kicked it down on top of my father's head.

"Now I want two medium sized forkfuls for the front corners, and the same for the back two corners. Now give me four more medium-sized forkfuls."

"Now" said Tommie, "You can give as big a forkful as you can lift, to fill the centre."

Slowly it dawned on me why I could not make a proper load. I could just imagine what I would hear if I kicked the hay down on top of my father's head. He would heave great loads of hay on top of my head and before I could climb out of this one he had another on top of me. It was a good feeling that it was not always my fault if the loads of hay were falling.

The making of a load of oats was a much more simple operation and I used to be able to do these as good as the next man, even though I was under ten years of age. Father used to mow the harvest with a scythe, and I used to take out the sheaves. In mowing oats the swathe was moved in against the standing crop and the taker-out got his right hand over the cut crop, and with his left hand on the bottom he took a hold of the cut crop and pulled it forward for about three lifts to make a reasonable sized sheaf.

Sometimes the sheaf would be tied at this time, but my father was a very efficient mower and it was more than I could do to take the oats out from him. When I was very young, my sister used to join in and between us we could clear the swathe in front of him.

Tying the oats was a fairly skilled job. You stood behind the sheaf with the grain on your right hand side. You grabbed about ten or twelve straws in your right hand and you pushed your right hand under the sheaf still holding the band. You took a hold on the cut end of the band with your left hand, at the same time you caught a hold of the grain end of the band with the index finger and thumb of your left hand. Now you pulled the grain end still hooked on your left hand, with your right hand until it was tight. You gave one twist with the grain end still held in your left hand, and you pushed the knot under the band. Finally you turned the sheaf so that the knot faced the ground. Later when you picked up the sheaves for stoking, the knot on the sheaf was on the inside of the stook.

One of the most pleasant jobs about the harvesting of oats was thatching the stacks. Building the stacks was a highly skilled job not trusted to youthful workers. Father used to do this work himself and I used to pitch the sheaves up to him. He crawled about on his knees in a circle about three feet in from the outside. The great principal was to keep the centre of the stack always well filled. In this way the straws were positioned so that if any rain or water ever got into the stack the water would flow outwards and not in towards where the grain and the most important part of the produce was. The shape that the bottom of the sheaves took while stoked, was such that up as far as the skivel you turned these upwards. This had the effect of leading the stack to become wider from the bottom until it reached the skivel.

At this point you turned the sheaves the other way so that it became narrower as you built up the stack until finally the stack was too narrow for a man to stay up there any longer and so the stack was often finished off a ladder, and a band of straw was tied around the top of the stack like a stook, and finally it was finished off with a forkful of green grass.

When the stacks had settled down after a month or two they were thatched with straw. The grain was thrashed with a flail or sometimes the grain was removed by scotching. Scotching was a simple enough job. You just took a good hold of a sheaf and swung the grain part against a large stone or the corner of a wall.

The flail was a more complex machine. It was composed of two parts –the handle or the 'colopaun' as it was known and the beater or the 'buailtin'. These two parts were tied together in such a way that allowed the buailtin to strike flat on the heads of oats to be thrashed. The operation of the flail required experience. My own memory is that when I applied the flail with full vigour that instead of the buailtin striking flat as it was supposed to, it hit the ground and then it flew back and hit the operator on the knuckles or on the back of his hand.

When the thatch was straightened out; it was tied in large sheaves, and was available for the thatching. The thatcher took a handful of this clean straw and stuck it into the side of the stack so that it hung down just below the skivel. Another row was put on in a similar manner and if a third layer was required it was also applied. Then a bundle of straw was opened and ropes were twisted. We used a stick about eighteen inches long, and I twisted this stick with the straw attached. Father fed in the straw so that a rope of about one and a half inches thick was produced. The length was a matter of judgement, but was approximately thirty yards long. This was then rolled into an oval shaped ball about four times the size of a rugby football.

When these ropes were laid evenly along the stack and kept in place by scallops cut from the sally bushes that grew in every garden in those days. Last of all the bottom of the thatch was cut evenly and so the stacks made a pretty picture. They were protected from the winter weather for as long as was necessary.

9

The February Fair in Kiltimagh

This fair was one of the most important events in our lives. It was at this fair that we, and indeed most of the people from the locality got their annual income. Long ago there was a train going northwards from Kiltimagh, and cattle buyers from all across the north of Ireland came to buy cattle and they could load them on the wagons and take them away. These northern men gave a fair price for cattle and they were very welcome in Kiltimagh.

Around about Christmas, Father used to set about preparing his stock for this fair. He would fill up the big pot with about four stone of potatoes, and put them on the fire to boil, but as soon as the potatoes came to the boil, he took them off the fire and left them to cool. Later he would chop up about a half a tub of potatoes for each animal, and he would add a few mams of rolled oats to each. Apparently it was discovered that cattle could take a lot more of these "scalded" potatoes, than they could if they ate them raw.

Five or six weeks was long enough to have these animals on this supplement, any longer and the hair would begin to fall off the animal's hind quarters. The men from the north never asked what diet the animals were on; they just paid for them and went about their business. If you were selling smaller cattle in Kilkelly you had a different sort of a buyer. He would nearly come home with you to view the mother of the animal and some of his siblings.
"Are you giving them the bucket?" they would ask.

The standard answer was, "Well, just a drink now and then." The first time that I went to this fair I was about ten years of age, and my interest was not confined to the price of cattle. I had never before been in any town except Kilkelly, and so to have been in Kiltimagh was a bit of a boast. Being up and about in the middle of the night was also a bit of a novelty.

"We'd want to be out on the road at about half past four," Father announced.

He had been up and had all the stock foddered, when he came in for breakfast. I had a lamp on the bike and I stood to turn the cattle out towards the tarred road. The animals moved very cautiously and some of them lowed in a low kind of sad tone as if they knew they were leaving forever. My mother came out to the main road with us. She pulled a red woollen hat down over my ears, and she turned up the collar of my jacket. She stood on the road wishing us God speed.

As soon as she was out of sight I took off the hat and put it on the carrier of the bike- a man couldn't be seen out in public with the like of that on his head. I sneaked on ahead of the cattle with the bike and I turned them over the Cahir road. The freezing fog was blowing from the west and it was right against us. I went up close to the animals and there was a bit of a break –their bodies kind of broke the wind.

As we went around Maire Aiteann's turn, I remember Father asked me if I knew what "aiteann" meant and I said that I thought it meant furze. He had the excuse that he never learnt any Irish in school, but he knew a lot more Irish than I did. He told me that Maire was a woman of the Kenny's whose husband had died in the later years of the famine. She had no land and in order to survive she started a butchering business, and she used to sell meat at fairs and markets or at any place where people assembled.

50

The fences were good along by P. D Kenny's, and the gates were closed, but as we came up to Lee's road a cyclist was about to emerge, and on seeing us he turned off his light on his bicycle. As soon as the cattle had passed the turn he fell into step with Father. His name was Johnnie Kilkenny, from Curhavnagh. Johnnie told me that I was a hardy fellow to be out of a morning like this without a stitch of a cap on my head.

The two men chatted about cattle and prices, and Johnnie stayed with us until we came to the Cahir cross, and then he cycled off towards the fair. There were people with cattle from Doogarry and Freehard and the whole group joined together as we moved closer.

The lights of the town seemed to come out to meet us and there seemed to me to be some heat coming from the great electric lights. By now the men's coats and the cattle all were white with the freezing fog. Suddenly the whole place became alive with men shouting.

"How much for the handlebars," one fellow shouted at my father, referring to our blue bullock.

"Do not talk to them fellows at all," Father said to me aside. "You see they are coming out to meet us thinking that they might meet some poor devil who does not know prices, and they'll get a bargain."

I was thinking that they wouldn't get anything soft from Father.

One of these buyers was coming very close to Father shouting, but father just kept walking along looking straight ahead.

"Well you could talk to the people at least," the buyer said, as he walked away.

"We made good time," said Father as we settled our cattle close to Walsh's corner. It was half past six and we had to wait a while for the pubs to open. As soon as they opened I got a steaming cup of Bovril. I was a new man after that.

51

Father stood by his stock careful not to miss any buyer interested in giving a good price. The buyers came, looked and shouted.

Then a small man in yellow boots wearing two overcoats asked in a low strange voice, "How much?"
Father gave him the price in an equally low voice. The small man looked again at the cattle and offered a price, but Father shook his head. "Here what's between ye – let ye divide."
"There will be no dividing," said he of the two coats, and he walked off.
"Here call him back – he won't come back again," someone shouted.
"If he wants these cattle he'll have to come back," said Father, as he looked off in the opposite direction. "I wonder did I do the right thing?" Father said to me.
I was flattered that I was being spoken to in this way, as if I were an adult. "He will come back again," I said.
"You take a bit of a walk around the town, and I'll wait to see if he does come back."

Up the street I saw Carrol's bookshop. This was the place where the master got our school books. I stood looking in the window, but the place was closed. I could see some great big books, and I fancied that I could get that delightful aroma that used to come from new books when they came to us in July.

When I came back Father had sold the cattle. The man with the two overcoats had come back. As soon as the bank opened he'd pay, and we were to drive the cattle up to the railway station. I felt kind of proud as I swaggered down the road from the railway station having accomplished what I came to do.

"Get a ham sandwich and some lemonade for yourself, and I'll see if I can get a lift home for you," Father said.

The first man I met when I went into Walsh's pub was Tom Donleavy, my next door neighbour. No kinder man ever came from Bruff than Tom. He bought for me a sandwich and big hunk of raisin cake and a bottle of lemonade. "When neighbours meet out they must always have a treat." That was Tom's way.

Just as I came out of Walsh's, Father had met Tom Nixon. Tom had a full load, but he was not going to let an old neighbour walk home. I got sitting in the front between the driver and front seat passenger. It was good to get sitting down in the brown leather seats of Tom's car. He brought me out through Knock, and in and out by-roads until finally he came to the Bruff cross. He was going down to pick up the master, and I could also go down and tell the latter all about the fair. I declined the offer and I got out at Neary's and walked in our own road.

10

A Little Grey Goose

As far back as I can remember there were always a few geese kept at our place at home. We never had more than ten or twelve. But there was always a few of the large white geese amongst the gaggle. Most of the time the geese were left to fend for themselves, except for a month or two in the springtime when they would be or should be laying. At such times they were allowed to share in the hen's rations of boiled spuds and yellow meal. At most other times they were dogged up the fields to fend for themselves and eat grass or search out frogs or snails

When all the land was covered over with five or six feet of snow, the geese were given subsistence rations to tide them over the Emergency thus created. The other creatures of the countryside that were not domesticated drew close to the domicile of man, during this Emergency period. I remember seeing a "graineog" drink the milk out of the cat's saucer at the back of the cow house. The fox too, became tame and he drifted up close to the house, but had little welcome to get at our place.

The wild and shy song birds like the linnets and the gold finches became as tame as the red breasted robin. I remember that I used to make snares out of horse hair and set them up on a sod on a thorn bush in the hope of capturing these little beauties, but I only remember that I caught a tom tit, and I was glad enough to let that little fellow go for he would fight, and give a sore pinch with his sharp beak. Still it was a great time to be young and to make the acquaintance of these lovely little creatures that could only be glimpsed at other times out in the fields. Best of all the schools were closed for weeks.

In all of the excitement we hardly took any notice of a little grey goose that joined up with our stock of domesticated creatures. This goose was a little smaller than the rest of the geese, but it was lively and clean and healthy looking. It ate greedily and trotted off into the goose house to be locked up for the night.

When the snow cleared off, Mother spread the word amongst the women coming home from Mass that we had a visiting goose, but nobody came to claim it. As the days were getting long the geese reverted to their pristine diet of grass and slugs and frogs. However when the dog was called upon to do his job of chasing the geese away out of sight, it was noted that the little visitor used to rise up above the reach of the dog, and soon all the geese developed this trick of flying out of reach. Then one evening a big white goose arrived into the yard with three lively goslings. It was then obvious that our little grey goose was a little grey gander.

He was getting bolder too, for whenever anybody went close to the goslings he came at them with a hissing sound and flapping wings. As the goslings grew into the form of a goose, the little gander took a further interest in them and it seemed as if he were teaching them to develop the art of flying. All of the other geese it appeared took lessons and soon our whole gaggle would rise up into the heavens, and set off to plunder some man's stooks of oats. These air raids continued on into the potato digging season, but they always returned home often late into the night, and they were always present in the mornings.

Towards the end of the month of November, the whole gaggle were spending most of the day flying about, reconnoitring you might say. They were certainly doing an awful lot of gabbling as if there was not entire agreement amongst them. Then one Saturday evening just as the sun was setting in the appearance of a red ball, the whole lot of them rose up into the sky, and I watched them as they flew southwards to the highest point in the village, which was then known as Kenny's Hill. They lingered about there until the sun had disappeared for the day, and then about four of them rose up and flew towards the northeast.

Somehow I knew that I had seen the last of them. In the morning the geese were back and they were gaggling about as usual, but the little grey goose and the three young ones had gone. Our old geese became content to remain on the ground, and even the dog was never too severe on them after that.

11

Graduation

From the time that I had completed sixth class, I began to look forward to leaving off school. I had noted the change that came over boys once they had left school. I had seen a few of them outside the church of a Sunday, the way that they would light up a long cigarette,slip on their cycling clips andoff with them on their bikes like any of the men in the village. I had wondered at this degree of sophistication and self-confidence that came over them immediately after they had left off school. I had passed my thirteenth birthday, and I was big for my age, but I felt none of this self-confidence.

My people at home felt that I had wasted enough time at the old books, and they were anxious that I finish up as soon as possible. Father, I know was anxious to have a full-time helper on the land, and not just for a few days help at bringing in the cocks of hay, or a bit of help with the harvest. My mother, on the other hand, was anxious that I get a job, and get hold of a bit of money. These jobs at the hay or harvest would get done somehow. Her plan was for me to get some job that would pay a week's wages. She often mentioned a County Council sandpit that was near our house, and at which she had seen men no bigger than I was at twelve. She asked me what sort of a good-for-nothing was I that I would not call in to the ganger and ask him for a job.

I used to enjoy the activities at home-haymaking or taking out and tying the sheaves of oats. I did not see this as work, and I did not relish the thoughts of working in the sandpit for the County Council. I didn't know any of the men who worked in the sandpit, but I had an idea that they were tough old timers who had worked for years in England. I fancied that they'd make smart comments about me and that if I tried to retort they would laugh uproariously at me.

These thoughts put a damper on my future plans. I had made up my mind that if I were forced to go to work in the sandpit, I would only stay there long enough to earn the cost of going to England.

At school the master seemed to have a slightly different idea about my future. He had long since come to the conclusion that I was not going to be in the academic world. Ever since he had found out that I had neglected to write my English composition for a whole month, he declared that I could never catch up. It was not that I had been idle- I had used the time allocated to writing to learn off the questions in my catechism.

The circumstances in our house did not lend itself to spending time at study. So I took a pragmatic decision which I was never allowed to forget as long as I was in school, and even afterwards the master told other pupils that I had not written composition for a whole year. At the time he threatened to tell the parish priest on his next visit.

I was petrified for I had no idea of what sanctions might be imposed by the reverend visitor. The big parish priest came hurriedly into the school, and straight away he began to question us on catechism. I was lucky enough that the right questions came up and I had the answers. Suddenly the Priest began to beam all over, and he complimented me on my answering. I can still see the sly grin of the old master as he accepted the compliment on my behalf.

Once I had the Confirmation over, and the Primary certificate completed I was free at school. My curriculum was completed, and now I was in semi-retirement. A few of the weaker boys were assigned to me as tutor for sums and Irish reading. Sometimes if one of the fifth or sixth classes was having difficulties I would be called upon to help out. At such time the master would tell how he had hoped that if I had worked at my tasks I might have become a teacher to replace himself. But I had neglected my tasks, and I had not written English composition for months. With each telling the time was extended to a whole year.

So I had neglected my tasks, and it was too late to ever make up for this lost time. I had often envied Tommie Costello his skill in shaping red hot iron, and I would have liked to have become a blacksmith, but that too was impossible. I was learning very little in school, but I was really enjoying reading the loveliest book I think that was ever written – "A Lad of the O'Friels" and in Irish I was equally happy following Padraic O Connaire in his travels with his little black ass.

I had my fourteenth birthday in April, and so I was engaged full time at home. However Garda McLoughlin called to point out that I was required to attend school until the end of the quarter which was the end of June.
"That ould buck there below sent him," was how my father irreverently described the master.

So I took the summer holidays with all the rest of the pupils at school. However when the school re-opened I felt the loneliness. I remember one day I was alone digging potatoes with a graipe, and to rest my back I sat against a sod fence. I could hear the children out at play and the tears filled my eyes. If I could have gone back to school again I would not have wasted my time. But it was too late for me.

For the next year I felt ill-at-ease. I was supposed to behave as a man but really I was a child. My pals were mostly middle aged men who had to remain at home to mind an elderly father or mother. I longed to get back to some sort of education, and finally I persuaded my parents to allow me to attend the vocational school in Ballyhaunis.

12

Origin

All of my ancestors hailed from East Mayo, except one, my maternal grandmother, who was born in England. Her father was born in Co. Westmeath, and her mother was born in the Co. Louth. My western ancestors lived on small farms of poor land. Each year they crossed the Irish Sea and they hired themselves out to farmers in England for the working season. Usually they returned home for Christmas, and if there were any celebrations they could drink a mug of porter as good as the next man. The one exception to this was my paternal great grandfather, Mickie Coen. He seems to have been an autodidactic in his youth. He spent some time in Co. Waterford, where he worked with the Trappist monks, where he learnt how to grow vegetables and the art of draining wet lands.

In later years, Mickie married a woman of the McNicholas' from the Knock area. They moved to Bruff in the parish of Aghamore in 1840. They had six children and they lived through the worst years of the great famine, and to quote his daughter Mary "they never had to eat any of the Yellow Buck," by which name the imported maize meal was known. The local lore says Mickie could read and write in the English language, and he was often called upon by his neighbours who would tell him their story in Irish and he would write it out in English

These letters which Mickie used to write for his neighbours were often begging letters asking for time to pay the rent. At that time there seems to have been an amount of litigation, and in this case Mickie would write a statement in English for someone who could neither read nor speak in English. Mickie was no promoter of the English language. He named all of his fields in Irish by which names they are still known. He also used Irish as the language of everyday use. My uncle Pat spent his early years with his grandfather, and he told me himself that he never spoke a word of English until he went to school at the age of seven years.

So all of my ancestors earned their living, by the sweat of their brows. Nevertheless they had a respect for learning, although I have not come across any book that any of them might have had. It was said of many of the Coen family that they had above average intelligence. On my mother's side her grandfather, Mick Boyle, had gone past the second spelling book under the old hedge school system. He could write and speak English. He used to go to England with five or six men of the Boyle's from Aghamore, and he was the only one amongst them who could write a letter.

So I had no important relatives. No priest or school teacher from whom I might get information about any advancement of study beyond the national school. I did have many relatives in England and in the United States of America, and they could if they wished direct me towards work as a labourer. At school I may have shown some slight promise, and the local parish priest called me aside a few times and he told me to work hard at my books, and he promised that he would help me later on. However he had moved on before he could be of any help to me.

The school master had found out that I had neglected to write up my English composition for a few weeks. I had used this time to learn off questions in catechism. And the master had made a major issue out of this. He told me over and over again that since I had neglected my composition I could not now ever catch up. I believed what the master told me, and I took less interest in my books, and I became more involved in the work on the land at home. I got through the primary certificate, and I went up to the Bishop to be examined, and I was confirmed.

As far as school was concerned I had served my purpose. I had still one more year to go to school, before I reached the statutory age of fourteen years, and during this time I was engaged in helping the weaker boys in the lower classes. Normally boys of my age would be taught something of how to write a letter home from England. It was accepted that I could do this much and also that I would be able to read the numbers of the buses in England.

I was not being taught any new subjects, nor was I given any new books, but I was allowed to go along with the sixth class and refresh what I had learnt last year. The master's press was half-full of old school books and I would have loved to get my hands on some of them, but they were not for me, but for others. Reading was just a pleasure; it had no other purpose. I had fallen behind and I could not now ever catch up.

In one way I was looking forward to the day when I could leave off school. Already Father had jobs planned out that two men could do so much better than he could do himself. On my fourteenth birthday I left off school, but the local school Garda served a warning notice on my father under the School Attendance act. I was obliged to attend school until the end of the quarter.

After we had the potatoes dug that back-end, my father had a job laid out for us. He had applied for a grant to drain four acres of wet land at the back of our house. With a sharp spade and a line he opened drains in a grid fashion, twenty-two yards apart. He just cut two sods neatly off the tough grassy surface and he left these on one side. I followed with shovel and pick and I dug down to a depth of about two feet. I deposited the spoil on the opposite bank to where Father had put his sods.

To check that the water was flowing in the direction that it was supposed to flow Father walked along the bottom of the drain and he cleaned up any loose pieces. Then he made a small gullet of stone, and he packed the stones tight. I then filled up the drain with small stones to a depth of about one foot. Father then placed the sods that he had dug grassy side down, and he stamped them into position. With a shovel I filled back the spoil so that it formed into a narrow ridge along the field.

By the time this project was completed I could be said to have completed my post-primary education, and I would have been deemed to be capable of taking my place in line with navvies in any part of the English speaking world. Looking back I must say that I enjoyed this work. I remember I often came across old drains that had been put in place a hundred years previously. Sometimes I remember coming across little pools of trapped water, and when I'd see the flow I would dream that I had found a great well that would supply water for generations to come. Invariable the little pool ran dry in a few hours.

I also remember that I dug up a colony of hibernating frogs. The poor old things were slow and I thought a bit lazy, but soon they jumped off down the little stream of water.

When it was seen that I was fairly useful as a labourer I became in much demand amongst the local farming community. Generally I did not much enjoy this work. I had an idea that being thus employed lowered my social status. I had not much need for money on a personal level, for I had not started to smoke and a quarter pound of sweets once a week was my total expenditure. Socially, my life was fairly miserable. My companions were men over the age of forty years, and they took an occasional few pints of stout of a Sunday night, and they'd look into the dancehall – they were too old to participate. For the rest of the week they seemed to be happy telling and listening to bawdy stories. I never enjoyed this kind of conversation, and I never told any of those dirty stories.

The few boys of my own age were either going to a boarding school, or were serving an apprenticeship to some trade. They probably remembered our school days better than I did, and they seemed to be able to adapt to some of these stories in a way that was passable. I often thought that these pals of my own age laughed with a special glee whenever I became the subject of this new kind of adult humour.

I had been away from school for one year when I persuaded my parents to allow me to go to the vocational school in Ballyhaunis. I had an idea that I might become familiar with carpentry. Two of my uncles had been excellent carpenters, and I had some hope in this direction. The woodwork instructor was a cranky little man, and he spent a whole session telling us how to fix paper on to a bench. The major part of the lesson as I understood it was that thumb tacks were henceforth to be called drawing pins. The next day we sowed cabbage, and I did not need any lessons from the stout old fellow using the spade.

The head master gave us a lesson in Irish and I enjoyed this, and the next day he gave us a lecture on English poetry, and he recited a few verses of poetry with great feeling. Then he gave us a test on English writing, and when he read my little piece, he turned over the cover of my copybook to look at my name. Then the headmaster made a short speech which I have remembered ever since.
"You do not have to go to school to become educated. You can educate yourself if you read intelligently. "

This was the end of my third day at the vocational school, and I never went back there again. I packed my bag and I hurried down the back road. I got off the bicycle and I walked along slowly. So I could catch-up and I did not need to go to school to do it. From that day onwards I resolved to read any and every book that I could lay my hands on. There were few books available in our house, and I did not know where I could find some to read, but I kept trying. I used to get a chance to have a read out of the daily paper which was always on hand in a house where card playing went on. I remember that I read all the long court case which the poet Patrick Kavanagh had with some other newspaper. I also remember reading the court case which Mrs Maureen O'Carroll took against a company that sold peas purporting to have marrow fats.

Even to this day I cannot resist the temptation to buy a book that purports to teach and especially so if it is second hand and well dog-eared. I have a small lorry load of such books.

13

Bogeyman

In the leafy pleasant countryside where I grew up we had really only one problem. That was time; or the lack of it. We worked from daylight until dark so that we had no time for leisure. Almost everybody young and old was engaged in the struggle to produce food, and turf to heat our houses. In the long nights we were free to enjoy ourselves in the dark. You see we had no electricity in these truly dark days, but we learnt to enjoy ourselves in the dark.

The old people had stories about ghosts that wandered about the countryside in the darkness. These stories were told and added to with every telling so that many people were really terrified to go out of doors after darkness. These storytellers seemed to believe in the existence of these wandering spirits, but in spite of this most old people carried on with their work and they also ventured out of doors when the occasion arose.

Even in the most poverty stricken areas you will always find a privileged few. One such a privileged person was a fellow named Stephen Roe. He had his upbringing in a city and he came to our rural area as an adolescent. He had never done any work, and he claimed that he was not able to, and so he got away, without doing anything, except ridiculing the 'country yokels' as he styled his new-found companions.

Stephen was a glib talker, and he was loose of limb, so that he could jump longer and higher than any of us. He had been taught the rudiments of boxing and wrestling. He dressed well and so was popular with the girls. It was his sarcasm that was most biting, and I myself often felt the edge of his tongue. I tried to avoid his company as much as possible. Even during the hours of darkness I often sat alone by the side of a grassy bank for an hour or two, and then I would return home, and lie to the old folks that I had met one or two of the boys for awhile to chat.

Stephen laughed at most of things that we did. He really laughed himself silly when he heard that we used to cut the tails off all of the young female sheep.
"Eating a bleeding sheep's tail!"
This struck him as really funny. It would have been a waste of time to try to tell him why sheep's tails were cut off, for he knew so much more than "Bleeding Red Necks" as he sometimes referred to the citizens with whom he was now forced to live.

At that time in our part of the country reports of the sighting of fairies were frequent. I recall one elderly man who was on his way to Mass of a Sunday morning, and as the weather was dry he took a short cut over an old pathway and there in front of his eyes was this man of about three feet high leaning against the step leading into Kelly's well. The old man was a bit surprised to see a fairy out so early, for it was the habit of fairies in our parts not to get up very early.

The mention of this incident precipitated a long list of stories of sighting of fairies, and then a more serious debate ensued about another breed of secret residents. That is people who grew to about ten feet tall. Apparently the fairies had taken over the local forth from these very tall folks. A great battle went on every night for a whole winter until finally there was only one member of the tall tribe. He left, and crossed the river. The belief was that he had gone in search of a great army to clear off the fairies. It was said that if any of these tall people ever appeared again it would be near the end of the world.

After one of these sessions of storytelling I was often petrified, and I would run all the way home for fear of meeting the aforementioned people. Somehow Stephen got to hear of my fear and he made life difficult for me. As the man said it would be a fool who would not be afraid, but it was a coward to show his fear.

I remember one year there came a very wet summer, and people relied on hay as feeding for livestock and the quality of the hay was poor. In the autumn, the weather cleared up and every day was fine, and so people began haymaking again. They cut the grass off the headlands that were left around the tillage crops. This grass was spread out on the stubbles of the corn crops and soon it dried, and became good hay.

During the year I had given the Yank, Kelly, a hand with some of his work, and so to repay us he came up and he was helping us with the late haymaking. Whatever about work there was plenty of chat, for the Yank was a great teller of his experiences along the docks in New York. In the course of the few hours that he was with us he took off his broad-rimmed hat and his long black coat. He was so busy telling some tale that he went home and left his hat and big topcoat.

I got an order to take these garments back to Mr Kelly who was so kind as to help us. I was imagining what smart-aleck Stephen would say if I were to be seen passing along the road carrying the Yank's coat and his big hat. I tried to put his hat on my head and it fell down over my ears. This was surely a case for fun at my expense. Then I discovered that Mr Kelly had also left his hand rake and fork. I draped the big coat over the head of the rake, and I stuck the prongs of the fork into the hat. The impression given in the half-darkness was of a man with a hat of about ten feet tall. I had met no one along the road. I stood at the crossroads, and I peered across the road and I suspected that there was somebody there as it was a practise of a few of us youngsters to congregate around the crossroads. I moved around the road in a circle to ensure that I was seen, and then, I issued a deep-throated growl.

I could not see anybody moving about and I was just going to walk off towards the Yank's house when I heard a shrill cry. It was from Stephen, I knew his accent, for he reverted to his city twang when he was excited.

"The bogeyman! The bogeyman!" Stephen cried and then I heard him calling "Mammy, Mammy!" as he sped up the road at a speed never before reached by man.

I went along to a house where I saw a light, and there was a card game is session. I stood watching the card game for a little while, and then I heard some whimpering that sounded like a young dog that was locked out. I looked behind the row of burly figures seated around the table and then I saw that Mrs Walsh was holding something on her knee. I took the lighted candle off the dresser, and then I saw the brave Stephen sitting on Mrs Walsh's lap. He jumped up when he saw me.

"I'll be down the road with you," Stephen said, in a very subdued voice.

"Hold on there a minute, you had better loosen the string first," I replied.

"What bloody string?"

"The string that has you tied to Mrs Walsh's apron."

I never had any more trouble from Stephen, for all I had to do was to mention that apron.

69

14

Our Little White Horse

The first time that I saw our little white horse he was snow white. Horses are not born white, but horses that are born grey become white with the passing of years. So that I could extrapolate that at the time when we got him, our horse had reached middle age. But whatever his age was he was full of good humour, and he was showing off. I remember when Father brought him home from the fair and led him into the yard outside our back door, he was prancing about, and he was rearing up on his hind legs, and letting out every neigh out of him like a pedigree sire. To people not familiar with horses, he was a real terror, and even experienced horsemen treated him with caution until they got to know his antics.

His mane had been cropped short into a "v" shape, and his tail had been thinned out so that it looked like that of a mule or a donkey. Apparently he had been used as a harness pony, and so he had been trained to show off. Behind all that show we soon learned that he was as gentle as a lamb. We were told that his name was Tom, and soon if you mentioned Tom he would come trotting up to you to see if you had something for him to eat. His favorite was a good sized carrot, but he was thankful for even a small potato.

We had already a useful cob of a horse that was good at pulling in the ploughing, and so Tom was needed to trot along beside the heavy puller. However, Tom turned out to be such a willing and versatile worker that he was used for every job on the land, and he was especially useful at carting.

We did not have the skill or indeed the inclination to dress him up in the style to which he had become accustomed. His mane grew long and wild and unruly. Father cut his tail short like farm horses were dealt with. This made Tom look very short and stumpy. Apparently the previous owner used to clip Tom's body hair with hair clippers such as a barber uses to cut human hair. This treatment caused his hair to grow profusely, and it was always falling off. If you brushed your shoulder against his flank, you would be covered with this long white hair. Whenever I went astride of him I always used a big grain sack to cover his body to protect myself against this contamination with hair.

The great fun was when we brought Tom to the local blacksmith for shoeing. I gave the smith no warning of our horse's propensity for always shedding his hair, and so the smith pushed and shoved the creature in the course of his operations. The smith had at that time taken up engine repair work and so his overalls were saturated with grease, which provide good purchase for the loose hair. As always in such places there was present a fellow whose main purpose in life seemed to be to comment on the affairs of life.
"Be the holy, but did I not think that you were a snowman."
The smith was not amused, even when it was suggested that if he had put grease on his bald head he might have got a good head of hair even though that it would be white.

The next time that I went to book in Tom for his half yearly change of shoes, I was met with a cold reception that he was so busy that he might not be free to work on Tom for some time.

Father took exception to this un-neighbourly attitude on the part of the smith, so that he went especially into town to buy a rasp, which is a sort of a file for cutting down horses hooves. Horse shoes could be bought ready-made at the time, and so Father became a farrier.

71

It was not just Father but the whole family took to Tom. If you spoke to the postman whose name was also Tom, the little horse would stroll up to you expecting some little tit-bit. He was easy to control; the least notion of a fence was enough to hold Tom. I often saw just a line of string across a gateway and that was sufficient to inform him that this was forbidden territory.

He was with us about five years, and then one morning he had gone. The odd thing was that he had apparently walked through a wooden gate and smashed it into smithereens. You could see the track of his home-produced shoes. Riders were dispatched in every direction to try to locate Tom. This altered behavior alerted Father for he had heard of this condition, and he feared the damage that a mindless horse might do. All of the local villages and towns had been visited, but there was no trace of Tom. From over ten miles away we got tidings of a horse walking along the centre of the road heading for a big town.

The Gardaí had the body of an old white horse lying in the fair-green. He was the kind of animal that the travelling fraternity might have had, but they refused to acknowledge ownership. All that the Gardaí needed was that someone would take the body away and bury it. Sadly it was our own little horse. He was laid in an undignified heap on the side of the road.

As he had walked along the road to Claremorris, perhaps he could hear the proud call of his ancestors that had often assembled in that town when horses counted for more than they have become. We transported him home and we buried him in a soft field, and a majestic ash tree marks the spot where lies the most loyal and affectionate beast I have ever known.

15

Ploughing

I stood in off the track in a place where I could see to good advantage the whole of the new field. The low pounding of an engine caused me to look, and there I spotted a green tractor edging its way through the bushes that were growing out almost across the narrow road. The tractor turned off the roadway, and it came down the track close to where I was standing. I saw that there were three silvery ploughs carried high on the tractor. The tractor slowed down its speed and it turned sharply into the new field. The driver just lowered his ploughs and he drove off along by the fence at a good walking pace ploughing three sods as he went.

I tried to keep abreast of the machine, but it got to the end before I did and then it swung down along the end of the field with the ploughs carried high. He turned in by the opposite fence and he ploughed three more sods. I realised that he was not going to set up markers and open in the centre of the field as we used to do long ago.

Never before in the history of man had this field been ploughed. When I was a boy we used to cut and save turf on this ground, which we now have named our new field. I remember when there were two turf banks running along at right angles to the track, and very good turf it was. It was much cherished for baking bread. The sods used to reduce in size to about the size of a bar of Sunlight soap. Ever since I can remember Father used to say that the turf was cut out, but one year he just went off to another bog where there was a more plentiful supply, and turf was never again cut in the home-bog.

With the passing of years some of the bog holes fell in and rushes grew on the low wet places and sedge grew on the drier places. The river Moy was deepened, and some of its tributaries were also deepened. The nearest point of the river Moy is about twenty miles from our place, but I have noticed that all the streams seem to flow westwards towards the Moy and the sea.

In the slow natural way that water works, the level gradually lowered so that now the water table is down to the level of the gravel, and so the ground can be properly drained. The wide tyres of the tractor prevent it from sinking in places where no vegetation has grown. Here and there the roots of trees that grew five or six thousand years ago, become entangled in the silvery ploughs, but the plough jumps up out of the ground and dislodges these old roots, and then it is off again. The green tractor growls along like some prehistoric creature.

The sedge and rush roots make like a tough carpet layer of about three inches, and the ploughed sods come like long belts trailing after the ploughs, that remind me of the belt that went onto the threshing machine long ago. Occasionally these belts break off and hurriedly uncoil back in the exact position that they were in. But the tractor driver is alert, and reverses to re-plough this area again. The result is not pretty, and the effort resembles an attempt being made to make cocks as if it were hay.

Nevertheless we were satisfied that the long winter rains and frosts would civilise these sods into a reasonable fertile tilt for the growing of oats. It was good to have witnessed this ploughing which I felt was unique. It is not every day you see the land being ploughed for the first time in six thousand years. It is just possible that this land was ploughed before the bog grew on it. We do not have any evidence of such at present, but further west closer to the mouth of the Moy in the Ceide Fields there is such evidence.

I was once a ploughman myself, and I can still remember the joy of holding that plough, and guiding it with that sense of achievement which is now only experienced by so few. I walked into our biggest field. It is just slightly over five statute acres, and my father fed us- his family and many of the citizens of the nearby town - with the potatoes and turnips grown in the rich yellow soil in that smooth level field. I remember the last time that this field was ploughed with horses. It was here in this field that I made my début as a fourteen and a half year old ploughman. This field has never been ploughed with horses since I left my mark on it.

I was very proud that I was able to plough. I remember my uncle came down to our house on a visit, and took a walk out to see the land. He stood at the end of the field and he looked along the straight even furrows.
"You made a good job of this ploughing. "
"Not me the young fellow there," my father spoke up.
"He has brought some of the skill of the ould fellow. "
Their father and my grandfather was a champion ploughman.

Educated townsmen would not regard having ploughed a field with a team of horses, as being much of an achievement. Anybody could do it they might say. I remember at the time neighbours looked upon my ploughing as being worthwhile. One woman went a little too far in praising me and then she added, "Sure, Dad said that them horses would plough that field themselves."

Looking back over sixty years I feel good to walk across the smooth surface of this field. I feel that I have in a way signed my name on it. I think that I can understand how the air pilots of long ago felt as they guided their primitive aeroplanes high up amongst the woolly clouds in the sky.

16

Threshing

Often of a fine evening late in the month of October a soft wind carries with it a kind of lonely moaning sound. It is as if there is a sort of sadness in the air crying for the summer that is just gone. Sometimes I feel like joining in this melancholic mood, for I can remember many summers that have gone. Could this call coming in the wind be the sound of the threshing machine that used to do its rounds in October and again late in the spring time? I listen again and it seems that this haunting sound is drawing closer, and then I realise that it is no more extraordinary than my neighbour of about a mile away giving a last cut to his lawn.

How well do I remember the coming of the threshing machine? At the first sound of it I had a hay fork on my shoulder and I was off to join in the excitement. The threshing used to rival the annual carnival that we had at the end of the summer. Make no mistake about it the work at the threshing was fast and furious. Most men gave all the strength and skill that they had for the three or four hours that the thresher was in each haggard. Some men who seldom did much work on their home place stepped up at the thresher.

I joined the threshing work force when I was about fifteen years of age, and I was given a knife with which to cut the bands of the sheaves. It was a job where the work was light and fast, and best of all I was stationed on the top of the machine next to Mick who was one of the crew, a very important man- the professional, feeding the thresher. I became identified with this job, as none of the older men fancied climbing up on the top of this giddy, faded red wooden box that might be taken for an upper class hen house. Except for all the belts that were moving, it seemed in tandem with itself. Years later I was reminded of my threshing days when I spotted Mick with his white gloves directing traffic in O'Connell Street in Dublin.

I remember the first time that I saw the thresher coming to our house. I was about six years of age, and I was not allowed to wander about as I wanted to. I was confined to standing on a little flag of concrete outside our back door. I was forbidden go past this spot, but I could watch from afar. The blue smoking tractor went first, drawing the great tall red and pink wooden box with wheels. When the thresher was well into the haggard, it stopped, and the tractor came out and turned and faced in towards the thresher. Tom, the driver, got off his machine and from a box at the side of the thresher; he produced a big belt rolled up. Hurriedly he rolled out this belt. He put it on to a kind of a spool on the thresher that I had not noticed before. Then he put the other end onto a similar spool on the tractor. He moved about very rapidly while all of the neighbours who had been coming with their forks looked on.

I remember Tom very well. He smiled at me and he stopped to speak to me a few times. He was wearing a kind of footwear that I had never seen before. These high boots came up as far as his knees, and there were no laces on them. I remember thinking that he would have needed a very long pair of laces to lace them all the way up. I asked a few passers-by about these extraordinary boots, but grown-ups never would answer a question from a small boy. Later these boots became very common footwear, but Tom was the first person that I had ever seen wearing Wellington boots.

I think that Tom would have given me a civil answer, but he was so busy with all the chores he had to do with the machines. There was another matter which caused me some concern. When Tom was putting on the big belt, he left one twist on it. I wanted to go out and tell him, but that was out of bounds, so I asked one of the neighbours about this.

"He sets it up for the craic."

"Why?"

"Oh, for keeping the dust out of his eyes."

What could a man say to that?

I kept Tom under close observation, as he moved about kind of slowly now, looking here and there.

Tom gave his tractor a wind with a handle at the front on the tractor and it was then that there was a loud whistling noise, and dust rose up like a cloud, and when this cleared I could see all of the little small belts on the thrasher were all going in different directions it seemed. By this time some of the men were astride two of the stacks of oats, and one man was forking sheaves onto the wide platform on the top of the thresher. I watched Tom as he pulled a lever of some sort. There was a ring at the end of it and teeth on it like a small saw under the steering wheel of the tractor. Tom moved this in and out until finally satisfied, he gave a half smile, and then slowly and cautiously Tom left his blue tractor, and he climbed onto the platform, and stepped into a well specially set up for him.

Presently he was joined by another young man and this latter began to cut the bands on the sheaves. Suddenly Tom sprang into life and he took an armful of the loosened sheaves and he fed them into the hungry monster. The machine gave a loud cough, and then too it sprang into action, and sent straw cascading out through three boxes that I had noticed were moving up and down in a kind of a circular motion. They reminded me of a boy who used to move his fists in a similar manner inviting anybody to take him on in a fight.

Inside in our house the table was pulled out onto the middle of the floor, and the medium sized pot that we used to boil potatoes for the dinner was hanging on the crane over the fire. I took a peep in and it was filled with eggs down boiling.

"Are they nearly finished?" Mother shouted to my father as he passed by the door carrying an empty bag with a blue stripe. Father stopped and considered this for a few minutes, and then said "Twenty minutes."

Work on the thresher was not to be unnecessarily delayed, and my mother hoped to have the meal on the table, so that there would be no delay. Each man got two eggs, or as many more as he wanted. The remainder of the meal was bread and butter and gallons of tea, which came from about three tea pots that were commissioned for the purpose.

When the meal was over, and after a consultation with Michael, Tom decided to leave the thresher and the tractor at our place for the weekend. Imagine how excited I was to know that I would have the whole day on Sunday for surveying the tractor which was parked at the gable end of our house. The thresher too had possibilities if one could climb up the little ladder that was built onto the side of it.

Early on Monday morning before I left off for school Tom came and drove away the tractor and the thresher. Later that same day I was explaining to one of my class mates the wonders of this machinery. The Gander, (the nick-name that we used to refer to our dedicated teacher) came down on me heavily. She showed no interest in threshing machines nor was there anything about such machines on the "claroibre". Amongst some of my pals I professed to be an authority on threshing, but for his own reasons, Father did not invite the threshing crew into our place for the next ten years.

Instead he did his own threshing with his own handmade thresher. This is known as the flail. It consists of two pieces of rounded wood skilfully tied together, and it is a very efficient way of removing the grain from oats. The handle of the flail or the colopaun as it was known was a handle

79

somewhat similar to a straight handle for a shovel. The other component was the beater or buailtin. This was about a metre long and it was about of the thickness of a brush handle. This was made from a piece of blackthorn well-seasoned by being placed up the kitchen chimney for at least one winter. There was not so much pressure on the colopaun, but it was usually made from a piece of ash. These two component parts were tied together with a loop of approximately six inches. The ideal material for this connection was the hide of an old donkey well cured and then soaked in oil. In times of necessity the two parts were often tied together with a good quality string.

The operation of the flail required a lot of skill. You did not simply raise the implement straight over your head as you would use a pick axe or an axe. The swing was more akin to that of the golfer. You swung the implement over your head in a circular fashion so that the buailtin came down level on the sheaf to be thrashed. I often watched my father as he swung with great power and accuracy. Often when he was not present I tried to operate the thing myself. In the first few strokes I was doing fine, and then when I tried to work in a really sweeping fashion, the buailtin turned back on me, and blackened the back of my hand.

This operation with the flail removed the grain from where it had grown on the head of each stalk of corn, but there was a lot of work still to be done. The grain and the chaff and short pieces of broken straw were all mixed up together, and it was necessary to separate them. This operation was first done by passing the material through a large sized sieve, which held back the pieces of straw so that you were left with the grain and the chaff.

We used to then go up onto the flat roof of the cart-house, and with the back aperture open as well as the open door, a breeze always flowed through. By pouring the oats and the chaff down off the edge of the roof, the chaff was carried off with the wind. Now you had nothing left except the oats. If some of the oats were needed for seed, they were further passed through a fine sieve. This let the small grain pass through and you were left with the large grains. The many little belts that I had seen on the thrasher carried out all of this work simultaneously.

17

Easter Sunday

A small group of old men were strolling along the road on their way home from last Mass. A few of us young boys were tagging along behind them. The grown-ups had long since gone home on their bicycles. These few old men were some of their generation who had never learnt the art of bicycle riding. Those of us of the younger generation could ride a bicycle, but we were short on bicycles.

The conversation like the weather was dull and quiet. These old men never discussed politics in those times - I suspect that the subject was still a little raw. Religion was never discussed for everybody in that part of the country belonged to the same religion. Someone said that the winter was about over and that next Sunday would be Easter Sunday. It was high time that all the ploughing was finished. Someone said that Barney Lyons had his potatoes stuck, meaning that he had his crop of potatoes sown for the year. It was a bit early – the ground was still very cold.
"Do you think that he will have any crop of potatoes?"
"He was the first to have them sown last year too."

To change the subject Tom Ned intervened.
"Isn't it a wonderful thing that on an Easter morning the sun rises dancing in the sky," said Tom Ned, who was given to making short speeches of fact.
"Did you ever see it dancing?" asked the Yank, Kelly, in a sharp quick question. He was a small red-faced fellow, who was wearing a broad-rimmed hat that he had brought home from America.

Tom Ned seemed taken aback by the directness of the question, and he hesitated, and then answered, "Well no I never did see it myself, but lots of people have told me that they have seen the sun dancing."

Big Andy stood up on the road and he faced the Yank.

"In truth," he said, "I have often seen the sun dancing of an Easter morning, and I hope to see it again if God spares me."

"So you think that you saw the sun dancing, Andy?" said the Yank in a sarcastic voice.

"I know that I saw the sun dancing, and there is no thinking about it."

"It was just your eyes, and you got dazzled, and your simple faith that gave the impression that the sun was dancing." The Yank was trying to explain to the others, but at this time Andy was getting a bit hot under the collar. He had dropped the walking stick that he carried, and he seemed to become a foot taller than he had been as we were strolling along.

Luckily there was someone with enough sense to stop the row and he intervened.

"I know that you are right, Andy - we all do, but to settle the question once and for all let us all get up early next Sunday morning and see for ourselves."

"That'll do me," said Andy, in a low voice, as he picked up his stick.

I was telling the old people when I came home from Mass, and Father said that he often heard it said that the sun dances of an Easter Sunday morning, but that he never saw it himself. Mother was noncommittal. All she would say was maybe the sun dances and maybe it does not. She had never seen the sun dancing, and she had something else to do besides getting up and looking up at the sun.

"People might think that you had turned into a half idiot if they heard that you got up in the middle of the night and started looking up at the sun."

Father agreed to get up to see the sun rise if I'd call him. So the night before I took the alarm clock and I was up even before cock-crow. I got up in the dark and I pulled out the rakings of the fire and I got enough light to see that it was very early. I waited until the first light came in the window, and I called Father. Once he got his pipe going he was ready to take up the vigil and wait.

We stood behind the reek of turf looking across it to the horizon in the southeast. The air was thin and fresh. I remember my father saying that people with T. B. used to get up at day break just to breath the fresh air. The pigeons were cooing to one another on the bare ash trees. A sheep called a few times in a gentle voice to her lambs. No smoke came from any chimney except our own.

Father had nestled himself down into a half-sitting position on the reek of turf, but to my consternation he was just beside a loose sod. It was loose because I had made it loose. By withdrawing this sod of turf off the Frey you could find the cavity within where I hid my treasures of cigarettes and matches. If his foot got caught in a sod of turf, a breach of turf was likely to fall and reveal my secret hiding place.

I had found from experience that it was unsafe to keep such treasures in my pockets, for sometimes, without warning, I might be ordered to divest myself of my coat or trousers, so that some repairs could be carried out. On one such occasion I had five cigarettes and a half box of matches confiscated. In addition I was to be kept under closer scrutiny, and I was severely reprimanded.

"Do you know that I do believe that the sun is dancing? Look over the reek of turf and see if the sun isn't bouncing up and down," my father almost shouted, and then he spoke to me as if I were an adult. Then he tilted his cap down over his nose to concentrate his vision. I was so uneasy about what he might find a bit nearer home so to speak that I lost concentration of the rising sun

"Come on in out of there and eat ye'r breakfast –ye'll get yer death of cold." I heard my mother's voice ringing out in the silence of the morning. I was glad when I saw Father coming into the kitchen, and I asked my mother why she did not come out to see the sun dancing on this Easter morning.

"Do you not believe that the sun dances on this morning?" I put the direct question to her.
"If God wanted to take up the sun like a ball and hop it off the side of the blue mountain, He could do it, but I think God has more important things to be doing than codding around with the sun."

I was thinking that if sometime God did take a few minutes off and take the sun off the blue mountain, it would be something to watch.

Later I was telling my friends how I had got up to see the sun dancing, and they were all impressed. I am sure that none of them had the slightest doubt about the truth of what I told them. I never heard if the old men got up as they had promised. They, like my mother, knew that if God wished to make the sun dance He could do it. However, few wanted to question Him.

18

The Roar of the Crowd

One night recently I dreamt that I was home in Bruff, as a lad of sixteen or so. It was a Sunday afternoon in mid-summer. A local town team was to play our local club in a challenge match. From our house I could hear the cheers of the crowd and sometimes too I could hear the bouncing of the ball on the hard surface of the football field. From these sounds I could form a picture in my mind of the scene. The townies all decked out in their white togs with hooped socks and matching jerseys. One or two of them would, I fancied, be wearing shin-guards as was the fashion at the time. I could see them doing some warming-up exercises like "leap-frog" or perhaps tipping the ball around amongst themselves.

A few of our team would be fully togged out and warming up at the other goal-posts, but most of our team would be taking as much rest as they could and a few would be drawing heavily from an un-tipped player. Away from the football we, in our own way, kept holy the Sabbath day. A man would not take his team of horses and go out ploughing of a Sunday, but the same man might take his spade and sneak into his garden, and work there for the whole afternoon. Some of the clergy were very opposed to any form of work on a Sunday. On this matter at the time I would stand shoulder to shoulder with them.

Father on the other hand was a bit ambivalent on the question of working of a Sunday. On fine Sundays after dinner he'd make an announcement on the following lines. "I think that we'll drive down the sheep and have a look at them."

He knew very well that it was never a matter of just driving down the sheep. On hot days the sheep would be hiding under bushes with their lambs, others would be nestling in bunches of rushes down in the bog. They'd face in any direction, except down towards the house. When you had some down near the gate you turned back to get the rest, and by the time you had them corralled the first lot had gone back again.

I considered this gathering of the sheep to be work just the same as ploughing or cutting turf in the bog. Father had an answer for this.

"Sure, it's only a bit of running and you'd run a lot more after the ball up in the football field."

Strictly speaking he was right, but it was up in the football field I'd rather be. It was not that he intended to be unkind to me or to deprive me of a Sunday afternoon of enjoyment. Farming was the only recreation that he had, and he would often spend ten minutes viewing the flock of sheep from different angles. Then suddenly he'd wake up so to speak, and take a look up at the sky (he could tell the time by the sun more accurately than the clocks we had at the time).

"I'll turn them out, you had better be off."

"I might as well turn them up with you now," I'd protest.

"No, off with you now – you'll be long enough at home with the old men."

Without further delay I would scamper up across the fields and in a few minutes, I'd be crossing the furze hedge into the football field. The match would be in full session, and although there was not any score board I could tell by the silence and gloom of our spectators that the game was not going in our favour.

I had barely settled when the play stopped. One of our most prominent players had gone down injured. They got him to his feet, and then two of them forced him to bend at the hips down towards his feet for two or three times. This remedy apparently did not work, so they escorted him off the field.

"Give him a jersey," I heard someone shout, and I looked about to see who it was that was being conscripted onto the team. The jersey that had been stripped off the injured player was thrown over my head.

"But I have no stuff," I shouted, meaning that I had neither boots nor togs.

"You'll be alright," shouted the mentor over his shoulder as he ran up the sideline away from me. A man has to do what a man has to do. So I took a few paces across the sideline into the playing area.

Whenever the ball came near me I ran after it, and when someone else got the ball I ran after him. I was wearing my hob-nailed boots, with three rows of hob-nails along the sole of the boot, with a toe plate and tips on the heels. Anyone who has ever tried to run with such boots will testify that in order to run you must lift your feet high up off the ground, rather like a stylish harness pony only not so graceful. It took me some time to build up speed, and slowing down was also a gradual process.

Nevertheless I suspected that when a member of the opposing team heard me coming thundering close to him, he got rid of the ball. Shin-guards were not protection against my vicious-looking boots.

On one occasion when I was in full flight the ball came towards me with great force. I hit the ball dead-on with the toe-plate of my boot, and this returned force seemed to multiply the power behind it, so that the ball shot off like a bullet, and it rose up into the air. Then like an aeroplane gaining altitude it seemed to stand still for one, two or maybe three seconds, and then the ball began to drop slowly it seemed, and as if by magic a tiny breeze curled it over the bar. For a brief moment I didn't know where I was, and then

I realised that the cheer was for me. It was the loudest cheer of the day, and this was the only contribution that I had made. I had done my best and I had been lucky.

The need to earn a living and the vicissitudes of life kept me away from football, for a few years. I never played again. When circumstances allowed, I might have taken a part, but I just kept away. I did not even attend as a spectator, perhaps I was apprehensive that I might be conscripted again as a player. This danger has long since passed.

Sometimes just to familiarise myself with current affairs I look at football matches on the television. I noticed that they can kick the ball a lot farther than we could in the past. I remember one time when a fifty yards free kick was allowed, we had only one player who could give the ball a long kick. He was brought up from his full back position and he kicked the ball into Johnnie Rogers' field. Now you see players scoring points without any difficulty, just tipping the ball over from a fifty yards free.

Sometimes I admire the skill of some of the modern players. The way that some of them can pick up the ball while running at full speed. Their speed, and the way that they recover after being bounced up into the air like an empty bag. How do they just jump up and carry on as if nothing had happened to them? The roar of the crowd is just the same as it was always. I love to hear this, and then I sit and dream what might have been.

19

A Rare Specimen

One of the noblest men that I ever knew was known by the nickname of Tom Skhy. There is no record of why or when he became known by this name. His real name was rare enough, but then he himself was truly a rare specimen. He was tall, but not exceptionally so; he was weather-beaten and mostly bedraggled like the rest of his neighbours. His long thin face was dominated by his large nose; underneath this he grew a rather spare moustache. For a time after he sprouted his moustache he was named Hitler, but that name had long since been forgotten. His neighbours were ordinary small farmers, but there was nothing ordinary about Tom. He was indeed a very distinguished fellow. If you were talking to anybody from the other side of the town and mentioned your abode, invariably you got the question; "And what does Tom Skhy think of the weather down there."

Do you know that many a time you'd be a little ashamed of him? Sometimes the stories about him would be exaggerated. There is no lie in the story of the time that Tom had to go into hospital for a few weeks. The weather was fine and his brother and a few of the neighbours cut and saved his hay and they had it nice and tidy within in the shed when Tom came home out of hospital.

However after a week or two when Tom got back to form again, he carted the hay out to the field where it had grown. He built a stack of the hay right in the middle of the field. The near neighbours took little notice of Tom's antics, but strangers who happened to be passing along the road were flabbergasted to see a man carting out his hay. In the first place they were wondering what sort of a hospital it was that

Tom had attended, and secondly they were of an opinion that he was released too soon.

Then after a few years we were beginning to think that Tom was becoming like everybody else. He had given up bringing his turf home in a bag on the back of the bike, and he used to bring a whole cartload home at a time. He still maintained that it made good sense to cut the turf during the winter when it was soft. He would start cutting his turf in November and work nice and steady cutting, and often around the Christmas, he would be throwing up his turf.

When the wind blew from the northeast, people said it was too cold to snow. Then the local people remained indoors, except that they would make a quick run out to fetch in some turf to keep the fire blazing. At such a time if you peeped around the corner you would see Tom below on the high bog with his jacket and waistcoat off and he throwing up turf. The turf never came to anything because the frost cut it to pieces, and the March wind blew most of it away in dust.

To tell the truth, we were glad when we saw that Tom had not gone to the bog, for a whole year, and that he was becoming normal. "The tablets are working" we joked. But just when all seemed to be well, one evening when we were driving in the cows, didn't we spot Tom's old red cow Rosie and she fully rigged out with the horse's harness on her. You know the collar and hames and a back-band, and there was Tom and he harrowing a piece of potato-soil, and the cow pulling the harrow.

You'd be almost ashamed to tell anyone that you had seen such a sight, but there was not long to wait, for next day after dinner there was Tom and he having two cows yoked up, ploughing a piece of stubble. The news got around to the ears of the parish priest, but he knew enough of Tom Skhy not to tackle the matter himself. He wasn't sure if there was a breach of Canon law involved. Many years earlier he had done a post-graduate course in Canon law, but then that was a long time ago. He consulted the Local Garda Superintendent, and this latter, joked that he often heard that cows were sacred in India, but he could not say off-hand, if a breach of criminal law was involved.

After they had each consumed a few drams of Paddy's whiskey, they decided that this was a case appropriate in the first place for the Society for the Prevention of Cruelty to Animals.

In due course an officer of the aforementioned society arrived at the premises of Tom Skhy. Ploughing operations were in progress, but on seeing the visitor approach, Tom called a halt. The visitor was a dignified middle aged lady, who had spent most of her working life in England. Now at home, she had volunteered her services as a worker for the society. She explained the purpose of her visit, and Tom who prided himself in being a law abiding citizen, afforded the lady all opportunities to carry out her inspection.

The team remained stationary, and since Tom had earlier fortified them with a mash of boiled turnips and oats, they stood peacefully ruminating.
"Don't go too close behind that lady there, or she might take your photograph."
The lady just smiled inwardly, and she wondered about the quaint language of this gaunt old peasant.

The big old red cow moved her hind legs and then she gave out a strange croaking sound, and then she let fly with a fine spray of diluted cow's shit. The light brown coloured mixture struck the front of the lady's white upper garments and then proceeded to drip right down to her legs into her rubber boots.
"I told you to keep back from that old girl, it was them bleddy turnips that I gave her this morning, but don't worry you will dry out in the wind, and then you'll be sound."

The lady made a hasty retreat to get home and take a "boath", as she herself described it. Her clothing was a total write-off, for she could never get that awful smell off them. The society accepted no responsibility for the damaged clothing, and so Tom was allowed to carry on, and soon he grew tired of ploughing with cows, and he gave a few pounds to a local fellow who finished his ploughing with a tractor

20

Doing a bit at the Trade

Some members of our family were skilled with their hands. In the days gone by there was little opportunity for people to develop their potential. For the females there was absolutely nothing, except to become proficient in bread making or perhaps knitting. For a few men sometimes there was an opportunity to become a wood worker. Two of my uncles became carpenters, and they got work in England and America.

To know that these kinds of skills were or might be in the genes was an incentive to me to take an interest in the trades. There was a forge beside our school, and the ringing of the anvil was like sweet music compared to the irksome tasks that were set before us in school. We also learned about the blacksmith who worked under the spreading chestnut tree. His strong and sinewy hands were as strong as iron bands. But as I got a little older I discovered that the blacksmith trade was a closed shop, rather like some of the professions.

But there were still other trades. The carpentry trade might be possible, and there was also the trade of shoemaker. Either of these would have satisfied me, and I was wondering how the many jobs at home would get done, if I had to go off to serve an apprenticeship. One evening I was just walking along a little road, when I saw a man who had just finished making a bucket out of an old sheet of galvanised iron.

He showed me how he had cut out the bottom of the bucket and the circle was still visible in the unused part of the sheet of iron. He had a minimum amount of equipment. He had a small battered hammer, pliers and a device like the saddle of a bicycle, but it was made of iron. The shaft of this was stuck into the ground and he hammered his bucket to make it fit to hold water

"Here," he said. "Fill it with water to see if there is any leak."

There was no leak. I must say that I was impressed, and I was thinking of this genius for days. I could get a hammer easily enough, but the thing that he called his anvil might be hard to come by. I came to the conclusion that a pick axe with the handle stuck into the ground would improvise as an anvil. At the first opportunity I stuck the handle of a pick axe into the ground and it seemed on an initial trial to be adequate.

Father came across the pick axe in this unusual position, and he said it was lucky that he did for someone might have stumbled across it in the dark. I made no reply to his sharp look. I became aware that the craft of tinsmith was not held in high esteem in our household.

I once visited a tailor's premises. There were interesting gadgets there and I was a bit surprised at the way the tailor sewed dark coloured cloth with long stitches with white thread. It was when he jumped up onto the table, and he began to stitch at a speed I had never seen before that impressed me. However I felt that tailoring was not the sort of manly job that I would like to spend my life at. Afterwards when I saw my mother sitting beside the fire with a few of her cronies I suggested that one or two of them might jump up on the kitchen table and begin to sew like the tailor. Instead of treating my advice with the respect that I felt it deserved, I was publicly admonished for my impertinence. These older people become stuck in their ways. Older people are the same today - they think always that they know best.

As the years went by I became almost indispensable at home, until I was offered a job as an unskilled worker. Now

I was offered money, and the rule was that you should never refuse money. One job followed another, and so my life drifted from one thing to another, and I was never to serve an apprentice at any job. It became apparent to me that I would never reach the skill of the man who could make a bucket out of an old sheet of galvanised iron.

I never fully gave up the notion of becoming skilled in some trade. When chipboard first came on the market, I experimented with it and I made wardrobes and I ironed strips of veneer on to the raw edges. Some of my relatives flattered me a bit and they said that the articles were just like you'd buy in the shops. In my heart I knew that my work lacked that finish which a proper craftsman might do. I usually gave myself the excuse that I did not have the proper tools to enable me to put the finishing touches to my work. I took to working with rough timber, and I made wooden gates that were strong and usable.

In this later phase of my life I have become interested in the more refined aspects of woodworking. These German stores have sophisticated woodworking tools on offer from time to time. You must buy these tools when you see them, for if you leave them for a few days the offer is off. So I have learnt to buy these whenever I spot an offer. So far all that has happened is that I have cardboard boxes, I hardly know how many, with modern woodworking tools that I am afraid I may not be able to use. I am beginning to think that a hammer and a saw and a few nails are all the tools that I will ever need.

21

I Become Gainfully Employed

I was still at school when Fr. Horan came around to the houses in our parish to get signatures from every householder to the effect that they would accept the electricity. At the time there was a lot of talk about the danger of having live cables clipped on to the walls of your house, and then these wires being poked through a hole in the jamb of the door.

"Would you get a shock if you touched these wires?" was a standard question put to people in the know about such matters. The usual glib answer to this question was

"What do you want to be touching them for?"

It was not as if people from our parish had not seen and used electricity. For almost all of them had at some time in their lives lived in one of the cities in England or in the USA. Where the electricity came from, they did not know. You just pressed a switch and the light came on, but when you could see the poles and the wires on top of them and the wires going all the way right into the house; that was a bit frightening.

"The Lord save us, it could blow up the house."

The big question that my father had for Fr. Horan, was how much would it cost and could he afford to pay for it. Even if you spared the light you still had to pay this ground rent. So having consulted widely and having carefully reflected upon the matter, he gave Fr. Horan a firm no.

"But you see that if you stand in the way your neighbours will not be able to get the light either."

"But they do not want it - they told me so themselves, no later than yesterday."

"I am just after being at their houses and here are their signatures," said Fr. Horan about to hand Father the paper.

"I will take your word," said my father and also signed to accept the light.

A few years later the same Fr. Horan, described himself on American television as a simple country priest.

Time went by and people had almost forgotten all about the electricity, or the light as it was referred to. Then one morning when they were coming from Mass they saw big black greasy looking poles stacked, here and there on wide margins of the roadway.

So the ESB was coming and how will the people pay for it? Soon word went out that workmen were needed to dig holes and help to hoist these poles. The pay was good - it was five pounds a week; that was slightly more than was paid to the road workers.

I myself, was just seventeen years of age, but I told lies, and added a year to my age, and so I got an insurance card. I dressed up in my Sunday suit and I put on my white shirt and a collar and tie, and I cycled to Ballyhaunis. I found my way into George Delany's shop near the bridge. In an office at the back of the shop I found the ESB. There were three smart looking gentlemen, all dressed in their Sunday best. I sat at one side of the table and they asked me a few questions, about my previous experience.

I told them that I could dig potatoes and that I had cut some turf. They seemed to be happy enough with my replies, and then one of them looked at my good suit, and he said that the only work that he could offer was rough digging. I said that I would do my best, and so they told me to be in the yards outside the office at a few minutes before eight in the morning.

I took my bicycle and I cycled out of the town and down the road for a few miles and then I dismounted and I began to reflect upon my future. I had harboured the hope that somehow I might get another chance at schooling, but now my fate was sealed or so it seemed. It was only a temporary job, but somehow I felt that now I would be labelled as a digger of drains, or as in this case, holes in the ground. Once I heard an old man say that you should never be in a hurry to grab a hold of a spade or shovel for there would be nobody in a hurry to take it from you.

I put on a bit of a show of being pleased that I had a job to the folks at home. They were both very pleased. Father said that in his own time there were no jobs like the ESB to be had. He had got two weeks carting with the horse and cart, for the County Council, but after a week he was laid off because he was drawing the dole, and therefore was not certified as being unemployed.

I was in Delany's yard in good time, and I was assigned to work with a stout young man with dark curly hair. I took no part in the vulgar rough chat that was going on in the back of the truck, but I kept a sharp eye on the stout young man to whom I had been assigned. The lorry stopped outside Frank Niland's workshop in Mountain, and my charge hand got off there and he took a roll of black cable and a few small boxes with him. I tagged along and he gave me the roll of cable to carry. We walked down a narrow sand road leading to Johnnie Tigue's and then we crossed some fields and we came to a low house. Three others members of our team had assembled there and so we commenced work.

At least I was not going to dig holes although I was fully prepared to do so. I gathered up hammers and screws and the ubiquitous black cable, and I loaded them onto a hand cart. This was about the size of a donkey cart except that it was more lightly made and there were wheels on it a bit like bicycle wheels. We sailed off across the fields to Johnnie Tigues, and the curly haired fellow whose name was Joe O'Brien, put an extension ladder fully extended up to the gable end of Tigue's house. He climbed up to near the top rung and he made two marks with the rounded end of the hammer. When he came down off the ladder, he handed me the hammer and a big blunt chisel. He told me to cut two holes for the swan-necks where he had marked. I had never been up on a ladder except at the side of a haystack.

I took the two items and I climbed up the ladder, too afraid to look down. I kept an arm around the ladder and finally I got the hammer in my left hand. I found that the wall was soft once I had cut through the plaster on the outside. My hands were shaking and my legs were trembling, but somehow I got the job done. Slowly I came down off the ladder, and boy was I glad to have my feet on the ground once again.
"Wash out the holes," he said and he handed me a battered old can with some water.

One of my colleagues poured a handful of cement onto a piece of a slate, and with the end of the big chisel he mixed some water with it, and then he ran up the ladder carrying the slate laden with the mixed up cement. He poked some of the mixture into each of the holes that I had made. Then he shouted down for two swan-necks. Joe O'Brien, handed me two items with a green glass, sort of like a mug, and he told me to run up the ladder behind my colleague. Mission accomplished, and I came down the ladder slowly, remembering how a few years earlier I had thrown stones at similar items on the telegraph poles.

The next order I got was to bring up the vice key. Now I was really puzzled, but Joe was on hand and he gave me a thing which I would have felt was a pin to keep the sideboards of the cart together. The straight end of this instrument was used to push in the small stones which were used to pack the space around the stem of the swan-necks. I reasoned that although the chisel was blunt it would still be likely to split the stones instead of packing them into place. Later I learnt

100

that the real purpose of the vice key was to wind up a strong wire that was sometimes used to fix insulators onto the chimneys of houses that had no wall high enough to keep the live wires out of harm's way.

I spent the whole summer going about from house to house, up laneways and sometimes across the fields. Almost invariable we were made welcome at houses, but there were a few exceptions. Towards the end of the month of August, I was given back my insurance cards, and the gang moved off to Castleplunket in Co. Roscommon. So my income was once again down to nil. I remember the little brown envelope with my name written on it and the amount that I was due each week was four pounds, seventeen and two pence. The fiver was cut down by subscriptions for insurance.

A ceremony to mark the switch on was held in the local hall, but Fr. Horan was not there. The same priest could not be idle and so he went off to America and he collected a lot of money with which he intended to build a great dance hall to entertain the young people. The people of Aghamore felt that the hall should be in Aghamore, but as Fr. Horan had a house built in Tooreen he began to have the hall built there. The parish priest agreed. A protest was organised, but nobody took much notice, until the parish priest came out before Mass one Sunday and he pulled down the notice inviting the people to a monster meeting. Not only did the priest pull down the notice in public, but he also formally wiped his two big shoes on the paper as it lay on the ground.

This action provoked the people so that there was indeed a monster meeting with a representative of every house in the Aghamore section of the parish. The Bishop was called upon to make peace, and so two halls were built; one in Tooreen and a smaller one in Aghamore. The old parish priest moved to Cong, and Fr. Horan ran his hall fairly successfully. I remember my father took no part whatsoever in the protest.

It is a fight amongst themselves, he used to say. Every one of these protesters has a bone to pick with the parish priest. He was a bit silly, and a hot tempered man, but he'd fight on behalf of the people of his parish.

I missed the income from working, although I used to give the four pounds to my mother and I'd keep the odd money, for I had started smoking a few cigarettes. Being employed gave me a tiny bit of status as well. After we had the potatoes dug another ESB job opened up in Kiltimagh, and I applied. I was put into the same work as I had done previously, and now I was an experienced hand. After about a month I was appointed as a charge-hand with four men with me. They were all much older than me, and sometimes they'd embarrass me with the deference that they showed towards me. I made no mention of this little job to my friends at home, but the word got out and then they or some began to realise that I was not as big an idiot as they had thought.

Generally I got the full co-operation of the men who worked with me. One fellow was a well know musician and so he would go first into houses, on my list, and his presence gave us a good reception. Not every householder was so well disposed to the music world. Some men would have to emigrate to get work, and they would see us as having soft jobs on their own doorstep. I remember on one occasion we were met with outright hostility. We had just taken our ladders off the hand cart when this man arrived foaming at the mouth.

"Get off my property!" he shouted in a hostile manner.
I stood firm as he came running towards me, but he did not make any attempt to strike me, he told us to leave in no uncertain manner. I gave a nod that the ladders were to be put back on the cart. As we were walking away I shouted after him as much to annoy him as anything else.

"I see that you have a sheep in trouble down there, can we give you a hand?"

"I have been watching her all night and she can't have the lamb."

I walked down in the direction of the sheep and we both met beside the sheep.

"I will hold her by the head if you have a go at pulling the lamb," I told him.

I could see that he had no experience at the job and I suggested that he hold the sheep while I pulled.

"I have a good grip in my hands from the work that I do," I said.

In no time at all I had the lamb out on the ground and he seemed to be dead. I looked at the owner and I then took the lamb by the hind legs and I swung him over my head a few times and then I left the lamb down and he gave a bit of a sniff.

In five minutes we had two lambs out on the ground, and when we got them to suck the sheep he invited me to go up to the house and wash my hands. The men with the hand cart turned and followed us up to the house. We all sat down to a good feed of bacon and cabbage. The problem was that the land owner had a dispute with the gang putting up the poles, with the result that he had ordered them off his property. Nobody told me and so we walked into the dispute.

So pleased was our man that he went into the ESB office and told the head engineer that he had changed his mind and that now he would be taking the light and they could put the poles wherever was convenient. He also added that it was a great waste of talent to have me doing such a trivial job working for them, when I was such a well-trained farmer. This did not add much to my status with my employers. I was beginning to agree with the view of the farmer, and I was looking for a convenient way out.

22

A Modest Little Man

I knew Tim Cob and his wife well. They lived in a townland next to us. They were a modest family; they had no important relatives and they were not known much beyond the district where they lived. Tim was an insignificant looking little man not more than ten stone weight with a red face and a small black moustache. In fact he could be standing beside you and you'd hardly notice him. Everything about Tim was small. His wife was no heavyweight either, and his farm was a little over six acres or approximately a quarter of the size of the farms belonging to his neighbours.

Of course Cob was not his real surname, but his real surname was so numerous that to distinguish him from his neighbours he was christened after a farmer in England for whom he worked for the first ten years of his working life. He did not model his farming activities on the English methods of specialising in one crop. He followed the same line as his neighbours. He sowed some oats and some potatoes, and he reserved two acres for meadow. He organised his farm into six little fields of approximately one acre in each. He narrowed the sod fences so that he was able to add a foot or sometimes a foot and a half to the length and width of each field. That meant that the fences were narrow and perpendicular, and so his beasts never attempted to cross them.

The thing that made him so different from his neighbouring farmers was that he seemed always to have great luck. He could grow better crops, and his haggard was as full as most of his neighbours who farmed four times as much land. His animals too were always well fed. His black ass used to have a shine on his coat, even though the poor beast was often staked along a wide part of the grass margin on the roadside. Of an evening you could see Tim going along with his wheelbarrow and shovel gathering up the ass manure to make up some concoction to help grow vegetables in his garden.

The same garden seemed to have no end of treasures very early in the season, which Ann his wife used to sell at top price. Any time after Christmas she'd be off to town with a bag full of pale rhubarb which she would liquidate for cash. So pleased were these fairly well-off people from the town, with her products, that she used to sell them hen eggs at a higher price than was obtainable from the egg dealer. Later on she'd have fresh cabbages on offer, and new potatoes.
"Sure she is only picking up pennies," the neighbours used to comment when they saw Ann off almost every day with the ass cart almost full of fresh products. We used to dismiss their efforts, but all the same we did not like them very much.
"Wouldn't you hate them?" was how one honest woman expressed the sentiment.

Sometimes you'd seen Tim going off of a Sunday with his penknife nipping out the tall blackberry briars and gathering them in bundles, to be collected later with the ass and cart. He would clean off the thorns of these briars and leave the long trimmed briars up in a loft to season. In the long winter nights Tim would move into the cow shed which was warm with the heat of the animals and there he would weave these briars into fancy baskets to be offered to Ann's customers in the town.

The proceeds from these briars were all profit, but he also grew willows or rods as they were called. With these, Tim weaved baskets of a more durable nature, and he also sold some of the surplus of the crop at the market to facilitate thatcher's, for there were still a few houses with thatched roofs.

But Tim and Ann did not spend all of their time working; for God also blessed them with one child- a daughter. She grew into a comely maiden, and she seemed to have inherited the prudence of her parents. The years drifted on and Tim and Ann seemed to be fairly snug. Since she had no other siblings there was never any doubt, but that the daughter named Kate, would inherit the farm and carry on as her parents had done.

From the time that she was a teenager the question of what sort of a man she was to be on the lookout for was the subject of debate by her mother, with other women who had an interest in such matters. Indeed some neighbours enjoyed themselves and entertained one another with stories of the sort of a man who might fulfil the expectations of Ann and Tim.

The old folk were in no great hurry to have a strange man come to take over the place, but one winter Tim was struck with a bout of flu. A day in bed and he was no better and so it was decided that Tim was a case for the doctor, and this latter was notified early the following morning. All day they waited, but towards evening there was no sign of the doctor, and so Kate was dispatched on the bike to get some homely remedies. They boiled porter and served it hot to Tim and then they put extra clothing on his bed and they waited.

While they were waiting the doctor knocked on the half-open back door.
"Am I at the right house?"
"You are but you didn't come at the right time."
The doctor moved into the house and he stood at the table to continue the debate.
"I was delayed because everybody in the town is down with the flu."

"Yes and we waited and we had your fee there on the table, but when you did not turn up we had to spend money on home remedies, and you know that you can't get that or the likes of it for nothing."

Ann indicated a five nagin bottle full of a dark substance.

"I do not bargain about my fees," said the Doctor in a haughty voice.

"You can go out the way that you came in so, because that is all this left of the fee that was there this morning."

The doctor knew when he was beaten and so he took the pieces of silver and went up into the bedroom to examine Tim.

Tim made a full recovery from the flu, but he was weakened. He was allowed to have one raw egg a day but despite this, he seemed to have lost some of his former energy. One evening Ann called a formal meeting of the household. Since Tim had qualified for the old age pension, and she herself would qualify the following year it was time for Kate to think seriously of finding a husband who could take over.

"What sort of a man do you think I should look out for?"

"Suit yourself," said Tim. "One thing I am telling you is not to bring a man in here who is too fond of drink."

"A pioneer," said Kate who had a bit of a gra for a shop assistant who used to dress himself smartly.

"Don't go bringing any little town buckeenin here even if he is a pioneer," declared Ann.

"It is a bad dog that needs a muzzle," said Tim decisively.

Once the word went out there was no shortage of applicants, and Kate paraded them before Ann and Tim. None of them gained a second interview. Kate was on the point of giving up and resigning herself to remaining single. Since her father no longer attended to the selling of livestock it fell on Kate to try to do this work. They needed to sell a heifer, and Kate utterly hated the job. Big Martin Moran called to the house and asked to see the animal that was for sale, and he offered a low price.

"You think that because we don't go out very much that we don't know the price of cattle."
"You might be right there Missus," said Martin, "but I'll tell ye what I'll do; I will bring the animal to the mart and sell to the highest bidder. One member of the family can cycle up at ten or eleven o'clock and witness the sale, and if ye don't get as much as I am offering you now, I'll keep her myself."

They sat there around the fire chatting and drinking tea, and big Martin told of how he had been in England for twenty years, and he came home and bought a big place, but it was a very bad house and so he was now living in a caravan. "I was going to build a new house, but I thought that I'd wait until I see if I could get a wife and she could put her stamp on it," he told them. By this time big Martin had removed his woollen hat and his steel grey curly hair was falling over his forehead. Compared to Tim, Martin seemed to be a real hulk of a man with his enormous hands which he used to indicate and illustrate points that he was making.

"Isn't it a great wonder now that you never thought of looking out for a wife," said Ann, looking very intently at their visitor.
"To tell you the truth, missus, I have been on the lookout, but where can a fellow like me go to look for a wife. I was never much of a dancer, and in my line of work I don't meet many eligible women."
"I suppose you are right there, but we could help you out if you treat us well in the matter of that bit of business we are doing."
"Be gad now but that's a fair bargain, and I will keep my part of it," added Martin with a nod of approval.

On the morning of the mart Kate was there in good time and she had no trouble in picking out Big Martin Moran. Martin himself put the first bid on the heifer, and there was quick bidding which Kate could not understand. When they reached the price which Martin had first offered at the house, he added another pound to the price, and the heifer was knocked down to Martin.

A few evenings later Martin paid another visit to the Cobs, and this time he was dressed in a tweed jacket and light brown shoes

"Well Ann I have kept my part of the bargain and got you a good price for your heifer, but did you make any headway for me?"

"From what I can hear you have been doing a fairly good job yourself."

"What do you mean like?"

"Tim or me won't have any objections."

"Do you mean your Kate?" Martin reddened up to the gills - a sure sign of the honesty of any person.

"Did you hear that, Kate, and what do you say?"

"If he will have me," she whispered and ran into the back-kitchen.

"This is something that demands more than tea and I have the very thing outside in the car," said Martin.

A big bottle of whiskey Martin placed on the table, and even Ann herself took a small taste with a grain of sugar in a cup. The important matter of money was discussed, and Tim let it be known that Kate would have their house and the little place, which was small but a sweet biteen of land. No happier young couple or old couple could you meet in a day's walk.

23

Joe's Light

There was never any lack of work in our part of the country, but the problem was that there was no money. So when I got a few months work with the ESB, I felt very lucky to have a weekly salary. Most of the casual workers taken on by the ESB were engaged in digging holes in the ground into which poles to carry the electric wires were inserted. This was rough heavy work. I was given a job of helping to hang the insulated wires along the walls, and fitting a metre board inside the entrance door into which these insulated cables were connected.

So I was away from the digging and also I was clear of shouldering the stinking poles that were oozing out black creosote. Working with a hammer and chisel and fancy pliers was considered to be skilled work. Working with a shovel was considered fairly basic work and it was not held in high esteem in our locality. The facts of the matter were that I was working as an unskilled labourer, but it was impossible to make my friend Paddy Joe understand that. He had seen me climbing ladders and working with a hammer and chisel, and so far as he was concerned I was a skilled man.

He had two lights and a socket fitted in his house when the great "switch on" came.
Sometime later he was in town and he had seen a swan-neck outside light that lit up the whole yard. Could such a light be fitted in his own back-yard? Imagine all the work he could do if he could extend the day light for as long as he wished. He had some important relatives who visited him from the town. They had the benefits of the electricity for many years, and a proper light outside would do as he was hoping.

110

He introduced them to me as the local boy who had made good, and naturally who better to install the light than yours truly. They agreed, and when they had gone home Paddy Joe went down in the room and after about ten minutes he returned with a damp and musty twenty pound note. I was thinking that there might be many more such notes to have kept this one comfortable. Paddy Joe had a reputation of having "old money" kept down in the room for generations.

To make a long story short I was directed to cycle into the town at my earliest convenience to buy whatever was necessary to install a proper outside light. Other neighbours might have make-shift lights, but when Paddy Joe did some job about the farm it was commensurate with his reputation or at least the kind of a reputation which he fancied.

I told the man in the shop what I was going to do and so he put everything that I might need for such an enterprise into a bag. My problem was that I had never installed a light of any kind, for like most of my neighbours, I knew absolutely nothing about the job. The man in the shop gave me a few hints, and here and there I picked up enough information to make a start on the project. I was experienced at screwing things to a wall and so I satisfied Paddy Joe by screwing the thing up in the most strategic position that would show some light to persons entering the premises as well as back through the fields to enable him to take a quick look at the "outliers" before retiring to bed.

From my experience in the ESB I had always noted that two wires went everywhere together like Darby and Joan-positive and negative. So I would begin with two wires coming from the source of power. I would have three relevant points, the power, the switch and the light. Two wires had to go to each, and it was for me to ensure that this two wire idea was followed. Although I had told Paddy Joe that this was not a part of the work I did in the ESB, I still had to maintain a degree of confidence, which I did not feel.

The man in the shop had sold me a junction box which was about the size of a polish box, but it was made of plastic. When I took the lid off, I could see brass studs with a tiny little screw going into each. So I concluded that wires could be joined together by this means.

Finally I clipped the cable onto the wall, and into the light. I took a chance and I put one cable into the switch and I brought the other to the junction box. I just stuck one other wire into the switch and on to the junction. Now I had two wires in each direction, but which of them should be live? Like my people before, I said in the name of God I'd take out the fuse, and strip the coating off the two wires coming from the metre, and insert them into the junction box.

I had an idea that if the wires were crossed that when I put back the fuse and switched on the light in the kitchen, the fuse would blow, and Paddy Joe would have to dust down the old oil lamp which still hung from the ceiling, and light it. The next day I would have to go to town and get a new fuse. The very thought of such an eventuality had me sick to my stomach.

With a shaking hand I inserted the fuse and screwed it into position, and then switched on the kitchen light.
"Is there any light outside?"I shouted to Paddy Joe.
"No," he said kind of lowly.
"Try the switch."
In the dullness of the evening you could see the light illuminated the whole yard.

We drank tea, and Paddy Joe produced a half a pound of fig roll biscuits, which he had especially for the occasion. We waited until it was fully dark to see the effect of the new light. He was in no hurry to tie in the cows for now he had a light and he could wait until midnight if necessary.

The novelty of the big light never wore off for Paddy Joe. He knew that from now on he could carry on with his work about the yard at any time during the night. In the evenings when he went out socialising, he always switched on Joe's light, to welcome him home.

24

Make Hay

While the Sun Shines

The sycamores have spread out long heavy branches reaching half-way across the stack garden. Years ago Father planted these to give shelter to the stacks of hay and oats from the violent northwest wind that sometimes invaded our territory. At school we learnt that haggard was the proper name for the stack-garden and in Irish it was to be called an 'iochlan'. To me it will always be known as the stack-garden.

There are no stacks in the garden now and there has not been any stacks for many a year. There is only there just a derelict old hay shed. Although the trees are old their leaves are fresh and young, and they offer me a welcome shelter from the sweltering June day sun.

From my comfortable seat I am peering out from beneath the spreading trees. The blackbirds and thrushes too are competing with their old time and still charming songs. No sounds of humans reach me, and as I scan the vast undulating landscape, no humankind can I see. The scene bears traces that humans have recently been here. The green fields have recently been plundered, and some have been shaved to a pale almost white colour. Some dark-brown fields have yet to be visited. A few fields of deep green have almost fully recovered.

This work of shaving the field seem as if it is done by stealth. Now you look and all is the same and then as if with the blinking of an eye all is changed. Now as I view I see curving rows of dark-green swards of grass, showing as a contrast to the pale-green of the mown area. I remember my father used to mow swards with the scythe with the same curvature. Sometime unseen man and machine will come and roll up these curved swards into a coil to be dressed in its winter coat of black shining plastic.

Long ago these curving swards would be tackled by men often dressed in white shirts. Early in the morning, they would raise the green grass high above their heads to spread out the grass under the sun. In another part of the same field women in gay colours would work no less diligently spreading out the grass. Each day they worked at the hay until it had changed into a light-brown colour, and then when there was a bit of a "rattle in it" they would all help to gather it into windrows. With a two pronged fork and wooden rake they worked without respite until the last of that field of hay built into field cocks.

Now the field looks clean and swept, and each cock is the same size and arranged in straight rows. A man could sit in a shady nook to rest, and be proud of his field of cocks. All of the hard work was instantly forgotten, and the next job was tackled with a will. In my younger days we did not have a hay-shed and so we had to ensure that on the day of bringing home the hay, it would not rain. It took at least a hundred cocks to make a haystack in the garden so it was a full day's work. If rain came when the hay stack was half way built it was impossible to cover it against the downpour.

We had what we called a "brath" for covering the hay. This was made by splitting a few pulp bags and sewing them together. Pulp was a bulky light material so that its sack was the biggest available. In my years working on the land at home I never saw us ever to embark upon a task such as bringing in the hay without invoking the name of the almighty God. My mother was more open about prayers, and between her and my father, they persuaded God to keep the rain away until we had the hay stack headed. I remember that it rained a half a mile away, but the rain was switched off to allow us time to head the haystack. I have no doubt that God did look after his people. The year's crop of hay was vital to the small farmers in those days.

I heard a story of a family who had a whole field of hay in windrows, and when they went down to the entrance of the field where they were to begin cocking the hay they discovered that the mother of the family who had been sick had come to see the work and she apparently sat down in the hay and there she died.

What were they to do? The whole field of hay in windrows - it was most vulnerable to the weather - it would be a complete loss if they left the hay in that state. The mother was dead and so a decision was made they would cock up the field of hay, and then proceed with notifying the neighbours. It is likely that God understood, but some of the neighbours got a whisper which aroused a suspicion which the family were never allowed to forget.

25

I Laugh to Think of It

In recent times I think that we people who live in rural areas, have become a little too refined. What I mean is that years ago you could go out of a summer evening and be entertained by two neighbours a half a mile away, having a good argument. Later on in the night you could hear people laughing for miles around.

This was part of the freedom which we country people enjoyed. Stifled whispering or muttering, or indeed discrete puffing is no substitute for a loud laugh, and it has no place in a country area. This kind of behaviour may be necessary in urban areas where you can hear the man next door raking his fire the other side of the wall. A good loud laugh whenever possible is good for body and the soul.

The great poet Goldsmith once wrote of the, "loud laugh that spoke the vacant mind." For a man who was reared near Athlone and who once taught school in Roscommon; you'd expect more from him.

The loud laugh usually comes from a very astute mind. Frequent practise at laughing loudly and spontaneously is to be highly commendable to those who aspire to high office. In this as in most skills, practise makes even the least talented passable.

Developed and practised skills, in these matters comes in very answerable in later life especially if you take up work in the public service. I have noted over the years that persons in elevated positions in the public service often also have a hankering to become stand-up comedians, even if only in a small way.

A shrewd junior who realises that his boss has this aspiration, can, if he acts sensibly, increase his chances of promotion by at least a hundred fold. All you need is to be able to predict when your boss is about to give birth to one of his jokes. It matters not that you have heard him tell the same joke a hundred times. To be able to throw your head back and render a wild outrageous peal of laughter is worth more than all the efficiencies that years of hard study can produce. But there are dangers. To laugh outright when the boss is making one of his pronouncements on policy, could end in disaster.

Many who hold top executive jobs today could claim that they owe their promotions to this clear ability to be able to discern when the boss needs to be supported in his aspirations for comedy. Conversely there are a few who misjudged and threw their head back and laughed loudly, when the boss intended to speak on official matters. There are others, who never learned to laugh in such a way that was appreciated by executives.

Though the stakes may be high, you should always be careful lest you do yourself an internal injury. Putting internal organs under unaccustomed pressure could do permanent damage. Constant practise, for example, is recommended when you are in the bathroom. You could try out your skills on a daily basis. Too early in the mornings or indeed too late at night are not the times to practise this routine, especially in urban areas. Some citizens are a bit fond of litigation, and you might leave yourself open, if you did not take into consideration the nocturnal habits of such neighbours.

As far as I can ascertain there are no academies in this country that purport to teach students the art of laughing out loud on demand as it were. There are, however, still pockets in very remote country areas where the natives still practise the art of throwing back their head and laughing out loud. Some years ago these people were famous for their ability at laughing. I heard of a much-travelled man from this locality who was walking down a street in New York late one night, when he heard a familiar loud laugh. He stopped and though the hour was late, he took courage and knocked on the door wherefrom he had heard the laughing. To his delight he had hit upon a group of his old neighbours who were having a reunion.

Unfortunately many of these remote rural areas are now depopulated, but it is possible that a few of the older people are still residing in rest homes and perhaps they could be enticed to give a rendering of the old style laughter.

Some of our universities have seen the need to instruct aspiring junior staff in appeasing those with clout. Professors have devised a course which is given through the extramural system, and these courses have had some successes. The essence of these courses is attention to detail. You know when you are bringing in the boss his mid-morning cup of tea, always use a cup and saucer, and for heaven's sake put the biscuits on a plate. If you must have tea yourself, always sup from a mug, and take the biscuits from the bag. Never, ever, sit down while the boss is having his tea. These little tricks show the boss that he is so very much above you. It demonstrates that he is almost a different species really.

There are still many old fashioned people in positions of influence, who prefer the rough sort of fellow who throws back his head and laughs heartily, at a good joke made by a person in authority. Many people, who have reached the top, seem to be comfortable once again to acknowledge their roots.

26

The Wonder of Spring

I pedalled along the hard shoulder of the bleak modern road. There was no discernable breeze, and yet when I got on the bicycle I seemed to be going into a head wind no matter what way I faced. The cold wet winter has lingered into the first days of the month of March. On each side of me I could see that the bare bleached fields were deserted. The usual occupants of these fields were still locked up in their filthy cells. In one low-lying field too impoverished to be ever grazed by a beef herd, I saw a lone bay coloured horse nibbling in between the rushes that grew profusely all over the field. He seemed to be sad and forlorn.

The horse raised its head and gave a low whine, as if appealing to me to set him free. My instinct told me that I should help to relieve the misery of this creature that is one of man's most loyal helpers. He might do as much for me if he could. I was up close to him and I could clearly see the big brown eyes so appealing. I fancied that he might trot off and pick up a few more of his kind and they would select a leader, and enjoy life as a horse might. But I have been disciplined so thoroughly that I ignored my instinct, and I slinked away like the spineless specimen that I have become.

Only the wild birds seem to be free, and a robin invisible even in the bare hawthorn, boldly gave out his restricted little performance. This little creature had survived the winter and was clearly declaring his confidence in the coming year. I turned off the main road and I proceeded along a narrow sheltered roadway. The cold air seemed to have mellowed, and then all at once I beheld a host of golden daffodils. I dismounted from my bike, and I stood in wonderment at such a display. The very sight, had for me, changed a cold and miserable day into a charming spring day.

On a clump of tall ash trees, crows were gossiping noisily. They too were in preparation for the coming spring. They do not rebuild their nests each year, they just refurbish them. Their smaller cousins, the jackdaws, were engineering a few chimneys still left without a guard. As I rode along I scrutinised all of the dwelling houses along the road side. I could not find a single chimney left without the modern guard that prevents the jackdaws from taking up his residence in the chimney flue to rear his family. I mentioned this omission to an acquaintance whom I met along the road. He looked at me steadily for an instant, and then he laughed thinking that I had made a joke.

These were some of the visible signs of spring, but what of all the activities going on unseen underground? Plants a few weeks later than the daffodils must now be getting a nudge to be prepared to face the bright new days. Tomorrow or in a few days we will see the result of these activities. Some new plants will appear all of a sudden over the ground. Without clock or calendar they will bloom on time.

The trees look bare and bedraggled after the long winter, and one of these days black buds will appear on the ash. The horse chestnut trees are loaded and one day soon they will burst out into leaves. The lilacs are beginning to show some leaves, and there in front of my eyes is the first flowering cherry with its flowers braving the winter winds. These things have been happening since the beginning of time and we still have enough faith to believe that the flowers will grow again and that the leaves will once again come on the trees.

I might have reclined on my couch to reflect again on the golden daffodils like the great poet who once came across a host of golden daffodils, but I have come from a different class. My memory goes back to a cold spring's day when a young man came to visit our house. He had come to make an announcement. He stood on the headland of the field where Father was working. He spat out into the cold wind and he kicked up stones, and he pressed some down into the soft soil. He was about to walk away, but then he stood still, and he spat a dry spit, and then he came out with what he wanted to say.

"Be Gad you know it's the end of February, and it's time to be making a start ploughing."

The problem was that our mare was unwell and not yet fit to yoke to the plough to accompany his own animal, and he was going to form a new alliance. This was a serious matter for my father, who could not form any new alliance at such time of the year. Our two families had been friends for several generations, but like business everywhere there was no room for sentiment. It was a hard tough world.

These were the memories that came into my mind as I reached home. The question of reclining upon a couch and reflecting on the beauty of the daffodils would have to be deferred until after sunset. To recline on your couch while the sun was up in the sky was unacceptable in the society in which I was reared. You would not be allowed to recline before sunset, except in case of serious illness. So the course of action open to me was to become active. The best therapy for man is working in the soil. I was no more than ten minutes digging when a couple of jackdaws arrived on the roof of the house nearby. I am still wondering though, where they will build their nests in the future.

27

Holyhead, Here I Come

I was about two years working full time for the ESB, and I was becoming a bit restless. I had learnt all that there was to know in the job that I was in, and I was looking for a change. I had seen at close quarters how electricians worked, and I made some enquiries about how one would become an electrician. All roads seemed to be blocked. I needed educational certificates in order to be accepted as an apprentice, and I did not have any. Further, there were age limits and all sorts of obstacles in the way. The next step in my own class as semi-skilled labourer was to become a linesman.

There was a vacancy for a linesman in Belmullet, and I was accepted. I had used climbers a few times, but I had no idea of what was required of me when I reached the top of the pole. I believed that courage was half the battle and I felt sure that I'd pick up the tricks of the trade. I was handed a pair of climbers and a long belt and I was told to go along in front of the gang that was pulling the three lines, and hang the wheels. I had never noticed such wheels before, but I walked along to the nearest pole and there I saw three wooden wheels with hooks on them - I presumed to hang on the cross-arms.

After I had gone what seemed to be miles I was taken in a small red van to go back behind the gang and carry up the three lines on my shoulder and place them into the wheels. It was tough work, and what was even worse was the fact that I was expected to be an experienced linesman, when in fact I had never before really climbed with these hooks that were welded onto the soles of my steel shoes. After a few weeks

123

during which I had eaten well but I do not believe that I put on any extra weight, for I often crossed over the bogs and mountains for distances of ten miles a day, I climbed every pole that I met along the way.

So far I had not made many mistakes. I could be observed going up and coming down the poles very slowly as was to be expected of a novice. Once the wheels had served their purpose, which was to ease the pull of the wires that were strung along this rough terrain, I was the man to take them down. Now I was to bind these wires on to the insulators on the cross-arms. Thick, single strands of flexible wire were used for this purpose, but it was not a matter of just tying it on any old way. There was a special method of arranging the wire so that one strand would not cut into any other. I was not actually sure of how this was done, so I asked a friendly colleague how to do it. He simply refused to tell me, but he did go directly to my superior, and he enlightened the latter, who called out one day and with the aid of a piece of string I was given a demonstration as to how the job was done.

In fact I never did know for certain how this was done, but I did have a prejudice against East Donegal men, or I had for some time. For the man who refused to spend about five minutes instructing me was a native of East Donegal. Two other colleagues were apparently experiencing difficulties at work. One evening after we were finished a job we were out walking (as if we did not get enough of walking) when someone mentioned that we should go to England to work. We all agreed. It was arranged that we would give in our notice of leaving the following Friday. So three of us handed in our company waders, and the official raincoat, and set our sights across the Irish Sea.

The question was - where would we go? My new bicycle was made in Birmingham, and so it was to Birmingham we would go. The train from Ballina to Dublin passed through Ballyhaunis, and when we stopped in my home town I hid in the toilet, for you would never how some neighbour might spot one on the train and word would get back to my parents. I did not tell them that I had given up a well-paid steady job and skipped off to England. I was so sick on the boat that I would not have cared if I had died, but I survived and got on the train to Birmingham.

It was about seven o'clock in the morning when we got off the train, and we looked about to see if there was some factory in which we might get employment. I fancied that I'd have a bit of a welcome in the bicycle factory, since I was riding one of their great bicycles. We asked a few people passing if they knew where we might get a job. They just looked vacantly at us, three fairly big young Paddies looking a bit dishevelled after the travelling. Finally one of us whose father was a member of the Garda Síochána, approached a young Police Sergeant, and asked him if he knew where we might look for work

I remember him well - he was a clean looking young fellow not much older than any of us. He had a job and he never took much notice where work might be had, but if we came along with him up to the station we could have a cup of tea and perhaps one of the older men might put us on the right track.
"We could measure you up for our job," he said, measuring all three of us with a look.

We thanked the decent policeman, and said that we'd look about for awhile, and then when we got to know the place we might take him up on his offer. Our next stop was to the bus station seeking to become bus conductors. We were well received there too, but the man said sensibly that it would be useful to know one's way about before becoming a bus conductor.

We judged that there was nothing to be had there in Birmingham, and so we set off on the bus for Bradford. One of our colleagues had a sister living in the city of Bradford, and he was sure that she would know where there were plenty of jobs. Instead of helping us to get work, she lectured all three of us. She demanded to know why we had left good steady jobs. Her brother accepted her interference, but two of us left and we got accommodation in a lodging house. We kept travelling until our money was nearly run out and then we approached the employment exchange where there were people looking for workers.

"Can you lay asphalt?"

"Yes sure I can." I had an idea that asphalt was a substance that came in sheets rolled up. The following morning at 6am we were to be out to meet the company bus. The landlady, where we were staying, was puzzled that we were to be out at 6am. Not since before the war had she heard of anybody going out to work at such an hour. She did not fancy getting up at about 5am to get our breakfast, and she did not trust us to get our own breakfast.

Our work was on an air force runway. We just stood around for the first week doing nothing. Then we were joined by a fellow who was named Sid. He was a tall lanky fellow who smoked Park Drive cigarettes and then he chewed gum. He had been in the war and he walked with a limp. He was a roller driver and therefore in a class far above mere asphalt layers.

Sid demanded a barrel into which we piled coke and lit a great fire. Not content with this Sid got a green cover and we made up a tent much like the tinkers used to live in. Next we were joined by the foreman, who spoke so little that it was not easy to know if he was a native, or an import like ourselves. Sid was very courteous to the foreman whose name was John.

Finally late one evening a lorry load of steaming hot tar arrived to be spread. So this was asphalt. My friend and I took two shovels and we spread the stuff about as directed by John. Sid was standing by with his roller which was not much bigger than a wheelbarrow. When he got the signal from John he moved out on his roller, and then he pulled off again.

"No bastard water."

My friend and I ran across the runway to a tap and we brought back four buckets of water.

When we had the load of hot stuff spread, John raked it around to level it before Sid came on with his roller. I grabbed another rake and I began to rake as I had often done in the hayfield. Night was coming on and I was well used to emergencies and so I raked at least as efficiently as John. When we had it all done, the agent, a creature I had never heard of before then, came over to me.

"You have been doing this work before now lad."

"Something very like it," I said.

"You are entitled to extra money for your skills, call into my office in the morning and I will organise it."

The same man had a company vehicle – a Bradford Van, I never saw the likes before, or since.

One time he needed some item from the other end of the runway over three miles away and he handed me the key to go down and fetch it. I told him that I had never driven a motor vehicle.

"You will never be in a better place to learn," he told me and got into the passenger seat and directed me. After that one lesson I was always on hand to take the van for any excuse.

Being a driver I was in line to take Sid's roller one day he was not in and I drove it. It went at about the same pace as old Isaac, so I was on familiar territory. One day Sid asked me if I would go down to the stores to fetch up some sacking. I hesitated for a moment and then John added, "a piece of a bag". Now I knew where John had come from. We used to have good fun with Sid. He would sometimes try to bully us a bit, and to put you in your place he would refer to you as Pat. We used to sometime play tricks on Sid and have him vexed, but at the same time we would always help him out with lifting buckets of water, for he seemed to be forever looking for water for the roller.

I was sorry when this job was completed, and the next job I got was on the buildings. I never claimed that I was a carpenter, but I did not say that I was not one either. I picked up an old saw in the stores and a well-worn three foot ruler. I did two weeks working with a fellow from India. Then a fellow from near home came around looking for union cards. I said that I'd bring mine in on Monday, but by then I was working on pipe-laying. My job was to keep a diesel engine filled with fuel and keep the welder supplied with welding rods.

I did all that was required of me. One time a very large pipe had to be welded all the way around and I dug a nice clean tunnel under the pipe for his convenience. Another welder had seen what I had done and he shouted "Here, Pa! Dig around this pipe too."

My boss got a bit angry. "His name is not Pa and he works with me."
"But you see my mate is not able to dig."
"Well then thee will have to dig it yourself."

That was the kind of loyalty that I experienced. This man introduced me to his union pals and got me so registered that in about two years I could go on a job as a welder. This man was a native of Bolton, which town was more familiar to my countrymen than was parts of East Donegal.

These English men did not profess to have any religious beliefs, but they were far more Christian than my acquaintances from home who would never miss Mass. The poverty that some people experience often makes them mean and selfish, any little bit of knowledge they have they keep it close so that their neighbour will not be as smart as they are.

If any of these English working men could help they were always ready to see justice done. I was in this job about six weeks, and now it expanded and many more people with skills in the steel industry arrived on buses. A wooden shed was erected as a store, and a store man was to be appointed. A general foreman was appointed and he brought a pal of his to act as store man. I was one of the first unskilled people on the job and so by convention I should be appointed as a store man. They got onto the union and so a stoppage of work was to follow to ensure that I got fair play. I was happier out in the open air and so I had the strike called off. I know that official England has treated the Irish very unfairly in the past, but I must say that I found the English working people to be the salt of the earth.

28

Building a New House

As far back as I can remember a subject for private debate around the fireside in our house was whether we should repair our old dwelling house or start on a new site and build a new house. The fact that we were a bit short of farm buildings was a factor that was given consideration. The old house would make a useful addition to the building already there. The government was offering a fairly substantial grant for the building of a new house, and the grant for the repair of an old house was not so good. At the time many people were getting out from under the wisp, and so there was a further urge to make a move. Our house was not thatched, but was roofed with galvanise, which was another factor in favour of building a new house.

At Christmas, Father had made a decision to go for it and build a new house. He went over Crockan Coll at the end of our land and he peeled off about six feet of the thin layer of the top soil to get down to the limestone gravel, and then he scraped down the face of the sandpit, and shovelled out the sand. He made the sand into a kind of miniature pyramid, so that the stones rolled down to the bottom of the pile. These were gathered with the shovel and put on one side for use as filling.

I had been working in England, and on the first day of April I returned home. By this time the pyramid of sand had developed into two or three smaller ones. We got a local man who had a tractor and a tipping trailer, and we conveyed the sand close to the site of the new house.
"Be the lord save us but ye must be going to build a skyscraper," was the comment when people saw the great heap of sand towering over the roof of the cowbyre.

Father had spoken to a local builder, and the deal was made. He would do all of the skilled labour, and Father and myself would do all of the labouring. The government grant was available and if there was money available the county council would match this amount. By being very careful these two grants would finance the materials for the house.

I remember the first day that we began working on the house. There was a lot of heavy work to be done, but I was young and I did not fear work. The senior partner of the father and son duo set out the rough outline of the house, and then he retired to the kitchen where he and my father drank a few bottles of stout. It was felt that there would be no luck in the house if it was not blessed with a few drinks. Like myself my mother showed her excitement, and she was talking about the layout of the kitchen. The senior partner, warmed up with a few bottles, told her, "Ah sure it will be a whole lot better than what you are used to."
My mother could give a reply to a comment like that in a flash and carry on with the conversation. I would reflect over such a comment for days and finally come up with a reply too late.

In our part of the country the laying of the foundations for a dwelling house was attended with great ceremony. The four corner stones would be placed in position, and if any of these were moved overnight a new site had to be chosen. In some cases many different sites were selected and each one did not pass the test. It was felt that if any of these corner stones were moved this proved that the house was in the path of the people from other worlds who roamed through the country by night. Many people gave up looking and they lived in the granary or in part of the old house while they were building the new house on the site of the old one.

We just got a ball of string and we drove down four pegs, and having checked for accuracy, we began to dig with spade shovel and pickaxe. In about a week we had mounds of clay and stones shovelled up. The conventional wisdom at the time was to dig a drain about two feet wide and keep digging until you came upon gravel. This was a problem for previous generations of the family had dug deep holes to get road making materials, and so we came across some of the rubble used to fill these holes. My father used to say that he had as much concrete underground as there was over-ground.

We filled up these drains with big stones and we shovelled in a small amount of concrete in through the stones, and then we finished this off with concrete floated on the top. Now the roofing timbers were delivered and we made up the casing with four five-inch-wide rafters. These were held together with short pieces of two-inches by one-inch lathes. The rafters would be used again, so the only waste was the lathes. These cases were eighteen feet long and I used to lift one end while the tradesman fixed his end into position while I held the other side in position. It took many of these lengths to go around the perimeter of the house. One day was taken to take off this frame for the concrete. The builder and I used to work on this, and Father was busy making stones available, and ensuring that the two barrels were full of water.

Early the next morning, we wheeled out five barrow loads of sand and threw them in a heap on the concrete slab that we had already made. Then one bag of cement was emptied on top of the pile of sand, and the whole lot was mixed twice dry and twice wet. This pile of wet concrete was then filled into buckets and I carried them and emptied them along the casing. Father was busy putting long stones into the casing, careful not to allow any part of the stone to touch the wooden framing. The builder was going about with a piece of two by one lath poking down the concrete. It used to take eight such mixings to fill the frame all the way around. When that job was done I was free for the rest of the evening except that I might have to drive cattle down to the shed and sometimes do the milking.

When the window spaces were left a little less concrete was needed, but then you had to climb a ladder and leave the buckets up on the scaffolding, as the building got higher. We were very scrupulous about not wasting anything. Nails were pulled and straightened and they were used again and again. Little pieces of timber were needed as spacers to keep the right width. These pieces were left in the wall. We used to snip branches off a sycamore tree that grew nearby and cut them to the required length.

In a relatively short time we had the walls of the house built, and before the autumn rains we had the slates in position. Now there was shelter and most of the inside work was skilled work like plastering, and doing the ceilings. Once we had the floors in situation, then the end was in sight. Sometimes when I was free from work I used to wander up the fields and reflect upon what I would do for the rest of my lifetime. I believed that I had an aptitude for this building business if I could find the right circumstances, but there was a narrow-mindedness prevalent, so that not only was it necessary to be able to do the job, you also needed some documentary evidence to prove that you were what you claimed to be.

I had written to the Government Publication sales office in the GPO for past Garda entrance examination papers. Having looked over these papers I felt that I might be able to get through this examination. The idea that someone who had never passed national school would consider sitting for the Garda examination was considered to be silly and to be unattainable. I had kept the promise that I had made to myself after I had left off school. I had read every book and paper that I could lay hands on in both English and also in Irish. My knowledge of Irish geography needed a bit of a brush up. The one obstacle was my handwriting. Being naturally left-handed I had been forced to write with my right hand and this perhaps added to my problems. Anyway I was almost seven years left off school, during which time I had written very little.

I wrote up a few compositions in English and in Irish of the required length, but I was too slow. So I bought a copy book, perhaps the first in seven years and I used to write something in this copybook each day. I carried this copybook about with me, and sometimes I would take a break in the bog and read over a little of the geography, and if when working a phrase that might suit in a composition came into my head, I would scribble it down.

I had checked my height and chest measurements, and I was satisfied that I was of the statutory measurements. So one day I called in to the local Garda station, and I spoke to the sergeant. Recruiting was not open just then, but the very minute that it did open he would let me know. I was happy enough with this and I began to write some more compositions, and learn off in a sort of a rhyme the counties and towns of Ireland. When we had the roof on the house I spotted in the local paper where a batch of recruits had passed out of the depot in Dublin. So recruiting had opened and I had not been notified 'the very minute' or, at all.

A retired Garda had opened a shop where we used to deal, and I mentioned to him what had happened to me. He told me that he got the paper every day, and he also passed by the Garda station each day, so that whenever recruiting for the Garda was open he would know and he would let me know. In due course the good man did cycle up to our house with the paper and the notice marked in red ink. He also told me when the Garda station was open. So I had my birth certificate, and my primary leaving certificate, and I presented them to the sergeant.

He stood up beside me and he judged that I was of the requisite height. He had a tape and he measured across my chest and I was of the requisite measurements. He then handed me an application form. As far as I can remember it was a fairly long form, and I filled it in, in a short time. He expressed some surprise that I was able to fill in the form, having regard to my background and education, as he had discovered it. He asked me how I knew that recruiting was open, and I told him that I had seen the notice in the Irish Independent, which was the God's truth.

End.

The Author Joe Coen

Born in 1937 in Aghamore in County Mayo, Joe Coen grew up in rural east Mayo. He had the usual experiences of young people of his time. He attended the local primary school until he reached the school leaving age of fourteen. From that time onwards he worked on his father's farm.

Joe did every job on the farm except shearing sheep. In one respect he outdid DeValera who claimed that he did every job on the land except ploughing. Joe became a ploughman at fifteen years of age and he ploughed with a team of horses for four or five years. He was also an experienced bog worker. He saved turf and cut it with the old fashioned slean. He was well used to driving a donkey in the rough soft bogs.

He finished full time education when he was fourteen years of age, but he became an avid reader; a reader of whatever he could lay his hands on. Books were not plentiful in his household nor were they available to him locally. At the age of eighteen he got a job with the ESB. A year later he went to work in England. He returned home and helped to build a family dwelling house.

At the age of twenty one years he applied for and was admitted as a member of An Garda Síochána. While working in Kildare he became aware of the second hand book shops on the Quays in Dublin. No visit to Dublin was complete without a few second hand books. These were mainly old text books on English and Irish language. He claims now that he could easily fill a good sized car trailer with books that are supposed to be good for him. The possession of all these books is just evidence that he had good intentions. It is not evidence that he has read them all.

Joe Coen worked as a Garda in Counties Carlow and Kildare and also Cavan and Leitrim, and then in 1967 he came to Co Roscommon as a Sergeant and he retired as a Sergeant in Roscommon town in 1990. He married Betty in 1966 and they had five children. Betty died in 2010, and now Joe lives lonely and alone in Roscommon.

(top) Joe and Betty, (below) Joe with siblings Tess and Bill and their parents Nora and Willie.

Printed in the USA
CPSIA information can be obtained
at www.ICGtesting.com
LVHW021330250823
756180LV00006B/578